ADVANCING THE BALL

LAW AND CURRENT EVENTS MASTERS
David Kairys, Series Editor

Also in this series:

Icarus in the Boardroom by David Skeel

In Search of Jefferson's Moose by David G. Post

In Brown's Wake by Martha Minow

Advancing The Ball

Race, Reformation, and the Quest for
Equal Coaching Opportunity in the NFL

N. JEREMI DURU

OXFORD
UNIVERSITY PRESS

2011

Oxford University Press, Inc., publishes works that further
Oxford University's objective of excellence
in research, scholarship, and education.

Oxford   New York
Auckland   Cape Town   Dar es Salaam   Hong Kong   Karachi
Kuala Lumpur   Madrid   Melbourne   Mexico   City   Nairobi
New Delhi   Shanghai   Taipei   Toronto

With offices in
Argentina   Austria   Brazil   Chile   Czech Republic   France   Greece
Guatemala   Hungary   Italy   Japan   Poland   Portugal   Singapore
South Korea   Switzerland   Thailand   Turkey   Ukraine   Vietnam

Published by Oxford University Press, Inc.
198 Madison Avenue, New York, NY 10016

www.oup.com

Oxford is a registered trademark of Oxford University Press

Library of Congress Marketing-in-Publication Data
Duru, N. Jeremi.
Advancing the ball : race, reformation, and the quest for equal coaching
opportunity in the NFL / N. Jeremi Duru.
p.   cm. — (Law and current events masters)
Includes index.
ISBN 978-0-19-973600-3
1. Discrimination in sports—United States—History—20th century.
2. Discrimination in employment—United States—History—20th century.
3. National Football League. 4. African American football coaches—History—20th century.
5. United States—Race relations—History—20th century. I. Title.
GV706.32D87   2011
796.332'64–dc22   2010017903

9 8 7 6 5 4 3 2 1

Printed in the United States of America
on acid-free paper

To Kanayo and Anikwe for Your Love and Laughter
To Mellissa for the Bicycle Card and
so Much More
And to My Parents, and the Rest of My
Wonderful Family, for Believing in Me

CONTENTS

FOREWORD
Tony Dungy

I CAN STILL REMEMBER the first National Football League game I ever saw in person. The Detroit Lions were playing a preseason game at home against the Cleveland Browns in the late summer of 1964. My dad took me to the game and, although it was nearly fifty years ago and I was only eight years old at the time, there are some things I remember like yesterday. I remember going to the ticket window and my dad deciding to pay four dollars to sit in the upper deck rather than six dollars to sit downstairs. I also remember that although we lived in Michigan and were definitely Lions fans, there was something about the Cleveland Browns that was special to my dad—there was some reason he wanted me to see the Browns.

I knew the Browns had a very good team that season—in fact, they would go on to win the NFL Championship Game (before it was called the Super Bowl). I knew he wanted me to see Jim Brown, the Cleveland running back he considered the best player to ever play the game. And I knew he wanted me to see Paul Warfield, the Browns' rookie receiver, who had been an All-American at Ohio State. He told me those things on the way to the game. But what he didn't explain at the time was why he and so many other African American dads were Cleveland Browns fans. I would find out much later in life that it was because of their history—because of their first coach, Paul Brown, and his willingness to sign black players when no one else would.

Paul Brown was a legendary high school coach in Ohio who went on to coach at Ohio State University and then, in 1946, became the coach of the Cleveland Browns. Brown had coached many great African American players at Massillon Washington High School and at Ohio State and made no apologies for playing to win. He didn't see anything wrong with signing and playing blacks if they were the best players at their position. When the Browns joined the NFL in 1950, that attitude gave them an advantage over the rest of the League, and they dominated the decade of the 1950s, playing in six straight championship games and winning the title three times.

I didn't know all that in 1964 as an eight-year-old watching the Browns play a preseason game. I just saw some African American players on both teams and at that point began dreaming of playing pro football. Those dreams, and my dad's encouragement, helped me to achieve that goal of playing in the NFL. In 1977 I made the Pittsburgh Steelers team as a free agent, and our second game of my rookie season was played in Cleveland against the Browns. My mom and dad drove down from Michigan for the game, and I couldn't help but think back to that night in Detroit with my dad thirteen years earlier. Before the warm-ups I went over and sat on the Browns bench, just to sit where Jim Brown would have. As fate would have it, we had two defensive backs get hurt during the game and I ended up playing cornerback for one series and covering . . . *Paul Warfield!*

While I had dreamed of playing in the NFL, I *never* dreamed of coaching in the NFL. It didn't seem to be a realistic goal at the time. Although in 1921 an African American named Fritz Pollard became a player/coach for the Akron Pros (which played in the league that would become the NFL), it was decided several years later that whatever jobs were available in professional football should go to whites.

Pollard and the League's other African Americans were forced out, and the NFL did not reintegrate until 1946. In the years following reintegration, NFL teams took note of the Browns' success with African American players, but unfortunately, that didn't carry over to the coaching ranks or the front office. Despite the fact that the NFL had seen many championship teams that featured African American players and America's professional baseball and basketball leagues had teams led by African American coaches, it would take forty-three years from the NFL's on-field reintegration for the League to see an African American head coach. Why did it take so long? In reality, there was simply a lack of opportunity. When I came into the NFL as a player there were no African American head coaches and only a handful of assistant coaches. There were no role models, no success stories. Most African Americans at that time felt if they wanted a career in coaching, it would have to be at the college level, not in the NFL.

When I was hired by Chuck Noll as an assistant coach for the Steelers in 1981 there were still fewer than a dozen minority assistant coaches in the League. George Young, the general manager of the New York Giants, told me that if I wanted to have a future in coaching I needed to shave my beard. He felt I didn't "look like a coach." George was a friend of mine, and he wasn't insulting me. He was trying to be helpful. He didn't know it, but his words really laid out the problem the NFL had been facing for years. There was a stereotype of what an NFL coach "looked like," and even if I shaved, I (and the other African American assistant coaches) still wouldn't fit the perception of what owners were looking for in their coaches.

Those perceptions would be slow to change, but several factors would help in that change. One was the work of people such as Al Davis and Dan Rooney, owners who felt that diversity was important for the League and who not only stated it but also acted upon it. Another was the entry into the League of a new wave of ownership—people who came into the NFL from the business world and who looked at human resource issues differently. And two huge factors were the formation of the Fritz Pollard Alliance, a group made up of minority coaches and front office personnel in the NFL, and the passage of the "Rooney Rule," which requires NFL teams to interview at least one minority candidate for head coaching and upper-level front office positions. The Fritz Pollard Alliance and the Rooney Rule created opportunity, and when given the opportunity, African Americans responded with successes. While there were no teams coached by African Americans in the first forty Super Bowls, the most recent four Super Bowls have featured four African American head coaches.

In January 2007 the Indianapolis Colts won Super Bowl XLI, making me the first African American to coach a team to a Super Bowl victory. Our opponents that night, the Chicago Bears, were coached by Lovie Smith, another African American. Many people saw that as a historic moment for the National Football League, and I was certainly proud to be part of that history.

I am very thankful that I was one of the people who benefited from the work of so many in this battle for diversity. I think you'll see through *Advancing the Ball* that because of the efforts of the Fritz Pollard Alliance, the NFL, and many determined individuals, while we are not finished in the journey to equal opportunity in the NFL, we have come a long way since that summer night in 1964 when the prospect of an eight-year-old African American boy becoming an NFL head coach seemed an impossibility.

ACKNOWLEDGMENTS

I COULD NOT HAVE WRITTEN THIS BOOK without the assistance and support of so many. I am deeply grateful to you all. Although I am concerned I may neglect to recognize one or more individuals who were crucial to this project (in which case I beg forgiveness), I must name names.

I would first like to thank Tony Dungy for speaking with me candidly about both bright and dark periods of his career and for agreeing, even in light of the seemingly innumerable demands on his time, to write the foreword to this book.

I would also like to thank Cyrus Mehri for enduring days and days of questions about minor details of events that unfolded years earlier. Cyrus never turned down an interview request and frequently rearranged his schedule to accommodate our meetings. His help has been invaluable.

Thanks also to John Wooten for his openness and, in particular, for sharing with me the deeply personal experiences that have molded his worldview. In addition, I'd like to thank Kellen Winslow, Harry

Carson, Craig Richardson, Jaki Lee, Gaynell Fenwick, and Steve Skalet for their insights and assistance.

Richard Lapchick has always been supportive of my work, including this endeavor. Thank you, Richard.

Throughout the process of researching and writing this book, the National Football League has been extremely helpful. I'm grateful to many at the League office for discussing with me what began as a difficult period in the League's history. In particular, I owe many thanks to Jeff Pash, who, when he did not have answers to my ceaseless questions, arranged meetings for me with those who did. Among those to whom Jeff directed me were Tom Williamson, Ray Anderson, Joe Browne, and Harold Henderson, all of whom were generous with their time and knowledge.

Writing this book exposed me to just how busy the NFL commissioner is, and I cannot thank Roger Goodell enough for making time in that schedule to share with me his thoughts and his hopes for his League.

Thanks also to Marvin Lewis and Terry Robiskie for taking my calls during the middle of the football season and answering my questions.

My colleagues at Temple University's James E. Beasley School of Law have been tremendously helpful as I've worked on this book. Thank you all. In particular, I must thank David Kairys, my neighbor on the sixth floor of Klein Hall. David saw promise in my idea when I had only a short proposal, and he counseled me as I transformed that idea into this book. I must also thank JoAnne Epps—my dean, but also my friend. Your support for this project has meant more to me than you know. Thanks also to JoAnne's predecessor, Robert Reinstein. Few academics are fortunate to have an extraordinary dean. I've had two in a row.

My research assistants for this book consistently put up with my scatterbrained system of assigning projects and my tight deadlines and still produced fabulous work. Clinton Albert, Laura Covey, Richard Diaz, Mike LaMare, Matt Luber, Ayo McAllister, Michelle Modery, Andrea Robertson, and Dongik Shin: I can't thank you enough.

In addition, I must thank my library liaison, Noa Kaumeheiwa, who seems capable of finding a copy of any newspaper article published at any time anywhere on earth. Thanks also to my younger brother, Chika Duru, who has developed into an excellent and exacting lawyer and who, despite the grueling hours of a second-year law firm associate, helped scrutinize both my original proposal and my final manuscript for typos.

I am fortunate that two of my closest friends, Khary Lazarre-White and Roger Fairfax, happen to be wonderful and accomplished writers. Thank you both for your constructive criticism on the manuscript as well as on so many previous writing projects.

I am also fortunate that two of the nation's leading race/sports/law scholars, Ken Shropshire and Tim Davis, have mentored me since I entered academia. I can't begin to explain how much I have learned from you both. I promise to pay it forward. Additional thanks to Ken for discussing with me his involvement with the Fritz Pollard Alliance and for tutoring me on the ins and outs of book publication.

Charles Ogletree was kind enough to share with me his recollections of his friendship with Johnnie Cochran, for which I am deeply appreciative.

I am indebted to the Honorable Damon J. Keith for the countless lessons he taught me during the year I spent clerking in his chambers. Those lessons continue to guide me both professionally and personally.

Oxford University Press has my enduring gratitude for taking on this project and supporting it through and through. Particular thanks go to my editor, Dave McBride, whose careful read and incisive observations greatly improved this book, and to Alexandra Dauler, for helping me to navigate the publication process.

Although I mentioned my family in the dedication at the beginning of this book, I cannot close these acknowledgments without another mention. From those who raised me to those I now raise, your love and support mean the world to me. I am truly blessed.

ADVANCING THE BALL

INTRODUCTION

ON FEBRUARY 2, 2007, two days before the National Football League's Super Bowl XLI, the game's opposing head coaches, Tony Dungy and Lovie Smith, posed together with the trophy the winning coach would hoist after the contest. The event should not have been particularly notable, but it was. Both coaches were African American, and that fact was as much a story as the game itself. Head coaching in the NFL had long been a whites-only business, and just a few years earlier such a matchup had been unthinkable. In 2002, however, two lawyers, Cyrus Mehri and Johnnie L. Cochran Jr., together with a few grizzled NFL veterans, launched a movement to expand head coaching opportunities that would profoundly change the League and, arguably, the nation.

Neither Mehri nor Cochran was involved in the NFL or its operations when they decided to challenge the League's employment practices. They knew as much about the League's inner workings as everyday fans, which is essentially what they were. Both loved the sport, and each spent his fair share of Sunday afternoons and Monday nights enjoying the NFL's product. But each also had grown to view that product as unacceptably flawed from an equal employment opportunity perspective. Opportunities generally abounded for African American players, but not for African Americans interested in leading them as head coaches. Indeed, in the League's eighty-plus-year history, African American head coaches numbered a mere six.

AMAZINGLY, DURING SOME OF AMERICA's most racially inflamed days, Frederick Douglass "Fritz" Pollard became the first. When Pollard made his playing debut with the Akron Pros Football Club, the nation was just narrowly removed from the infamous "Red Summer" of 1919, during which a frenzy of lynchings and other racial attacks left the African American community battered and shaken and American race relations at their most raw. A year later, the Pros joined the American Professional Football Association—later renamed the NFL—and somehow, a year after that, in spite of the racism overwhelming the nation, the Pros appointed Pollard as a co–head coach.

More than sixty years would pass before another African American held an NFL head coaching job. For several of those years, from 1934 to 1946, the League segregated, banning African Americans from its ranks altogether. But following desegregation in 1946, team owners increasingly hired African American players to stock their previously all-white rosters, and within a few decades African American players had grown to numerically dominate the League. Nevertheless, African Americans were virtually nonexistent among those who wielded power within the teams' structures and over their players.

In this respect the NFL was not entirely unlike America's other premier professional sports leagues. Major League Baseball owners and National Basketball Association owners, like NFL owners, seemed comfortable fielding scores of African American (and, in the case of Major League Baseball, Latino) players but were far less willing to hire a person of color to lead them.

Those other leagues, however, had shown signs of progress. The NBA featured its first head coach of color in 1966, and Major League Baseball saw its first manager of color in 1975; in both leagues, more would follow. In contrast, as of the 1989 NFL season's inception, although over 60 percent of the NFL's players were of color, all thirty-two NFL head coaches were white.

Debate as to why, precisely, the NFL's head coaching ranks were so uniquely colorless birthed multiple theories, the most damning of which attributed the League's long-standing head coaching homogeneity to a combination of centuries-old suppositions and the game's nature. Football is without question America's most complex sport. A football team's playbook can be up to several inches thick and generally contains seemingly innumerable formations and plays. But the playbook tells only part of the story. The game's complexity is most clearly evident as opposing teams prepare for any given play.

Having received instructions from their coaches and huddled up to discuss strategy, the players from both teams get into position. The defensive players array themselves in response to the offense's alignment, while the quarterback barks coded instructions. The instructions sometimes trigger movement from one of his teammates, and in the event of such movement, and even in its absence, the defense often adjusts its positioning. Based on the defense's repositioning, the quarterback sometimes gives new instructions, sparking another round of movement. All the while, a defensive player—often the middle linebacker—is issuing instructions of his own. Once the quarterback calls for the ball, all eleven offensive players execute carefully choreographed maneuvers, each reliant on the precision of his ten teammates. Their defensive counterparts, meanwhile, must respond with their own well-rehearsed schemes to thwart the particular play unfolding before them. When the play ends, each team gathers, regroups, and strategizes anew. Athleticism and instinct are, of course, fundamental to success on both sides of the ball, but without intense study and preparation of a scope unmatched in American sport, failure is certain.

The head coach is responsible for coordinating that study and ensuring that the players are prepared to execute; he must therefore be a master strategist and motivator. In addition, because football rosters are extremely large, featuring twice as many players as baseball rosters and four times as many as basketball rosters, a head football coach must be an adept personnel manager. Stereotypes of African American intellectual inferiority dating to slavery presupposed African Americans insufficiently cerebral to succeed in such roles. Some theorists held that NFL team owners, all of whom were white, shunned African American head coaching candidates because of conscious or subconscious reliance on those stereotypes.

Other theorists laid blame on a perhaps less malignant but no less damaging phenomenon: the old-boy network, which seemed to thrive in the NFL's generally conservative culture, and which resulted in friends hiring friends and friends of friends, all of whom happened to be white.

Despite the obstacles facing African Americans aspiring to NFL careers beyond the playing field, and whatever those obstacles' roots, a small number of African Americans had over the years secured positions in teams' front offices and on teams' coaching staffs, and they toiled to open off-field opportunities for others. Their agitation was professionally risky, of course. To some in the NFL, the racial status quo was just fine, and the concept of increased diversity was unsettling. But the League's few African American coaches and front office personnel were children of the civil rights movement and had seen people risk far more than professional security and advancement in pursuit of racial equality. They were undaunted, and they eventually made headway in the coaching realm, as during the late 1970s and the 1980s, teams seemed increasingly willing to appoint African Americans to their coaching staffs. Even so, the color barrier at the top of the coaching hierarchy—the barrier Pollard had surmounted sixty years earlier—remained intact.

Four games into the 1989 season, the Los Angeles Raiders' offensive line coach, Art Shell, broke through. The Raiders' storied franchise was struggling, and team owner Al Davis, knowing the organization needed a change, named Shell his head coach. Suddenly Shell symbolized the possibility of a new era in the NFL, one in which African Americans might just as reasonably dream of coaching a Super Bowl team as playing for one. But the new era's promise proved illusory, and by early 2002 frustration among the League's off-field African Americans was boiling. Shell, despite his success with the Raiders, had long since been terminated. And after the 2001 season, two of the four African Americans who had managed to land head coaching positions in the years after Shell did so were fired as well, despite substantial successes of their own.

Still other African Americans had compiled impeccable credentials as NFL assistant coaches over many years without ever receiving a head coaching opportunity. Sherman Lewis, for instance, had been an assistant coach in the League for fourteen years, during ten of which he served just under the head coach as offensive coordinator. He spent most of that time with the Green Bay Packers and was largely responsible for directing Brett Favre and the Packers' offense to two Super Bowl appearances and one Super Bowl victory. Yet he had generally been a head coaching afterthought. The same was true of Emmitt Thomas, who had been one of the NFL's most successful defensive backs during his playing days and who had proven himself as talented a defensive coach as Lewis was an offensive coach. Although Thomas was an NFL assistant coach for twenty-one years and although he spent seven of those years as a defensive coordinator producing consistently dominant defensive units, he too had been largely ignored for head coaching positions. Each year team officials from around the League praised Lewis and Thomas as exceptional coaches well suited for head coaching duties, but no head coaching offers ever attached.

In 2002 both men, having worked as assistants for years with little hope of advancement, were nearing sixty. It appeared unlikely that either would ever be an NFL head coach. And the younger generation, it seemed, would fare no better. After all, if the Baltimore Ravens' young and dynamic defensive coordinator, Marvin Lewis (no relation to Sherman), had not secured a head coaching job, prospects looked relatively bleak for the League's other African American assistant coaches.

Marvin Lewis had been a standout coach since entering the League in 1992, and upon joining the Ravens' coaching staff in 1996 he began systematically molding the team's defensive unit into a juggernaut. By 2000 he had crafted it into perhaps the best defense in NFL history. Overall, the Ravens were not a great team that year. Their offense was barely mediocre, and at one point during the season it went an astonishing five games without scoring a touchdown. Despite this, Lewis' defense was relentless, obliterating the NFL record for fewest points allowed in a season and leading the Ravens into the playoffs and ultimately to a Super Bowl Championship. As spectacular as Lewis' coaching career was, he, like Sherman Lewis, Emmitt Thomas, and so many other successful African American assistant coaches in the NFL, had never received a head coaching offer.

The inequity, and the "last hired, first fired" pattern it had produced, was glaring to every African American involved in the League, including those who decades earlier had initiated the push to diversify the League's coaching ranks. While some of those early activists had since left the League and others had passed away, a few were still active in NFL affairs, and they continued to carry the mantle, organizing and mentoring those who had entered the League after them and persisting with the campaign they had begun a quarter century earlier. John Wooten, a former Cleveland Browns offensive lineman, by then in his late sixties, led the effort.

Mehri and Cochran, at the time, knew nothing of Wooten and his work, but they were fed up with the NFL and vowed to change it. They set out to convince anyone who would listen that NFL teams were discriminating against African American head coaches and head coaching aspirants. Wooten and his closest allies, sensing the leverage Mehri and Cochran's efforts represented, offered their assistance, and the new coalition demanded that the NFL reform. By 2007, as Dungy and Smith prepared for their historic Super Bowl confrontation, the NFL had done just that. The League had implemented detailed regulations designed to thwart discrimination and myopia in its teams' head coach hiring processes, resulting in a dramatic increase in the number of African American head coaches. The NFL's transformation was unprecedented, and Dungy, Smith, and the League's other African American head coaches stood proudly as equal opportunity's yield.

More interesting even than the NFL's ultimate transformation is the struggle that propelled it—a struggle I had the good fortune to observe, and in small part aid, first as an attorney in Cyrus Mehri's law office and then as an activist academic. By way of unlikely alliances, legal brinksmanship, and grassroots organizing, a few committed individuals initiated a sea change in America's most popular and profitable sports league. Moreover, through successfully engaging one of America's most vexing societal problems in the country's most public forum, they opened a window into both the benefits of equal employment opportunity and the tools with which to secure it, thus providing fair-minded corporate CEOs, executives in other sports leagues, and organization heads of all sorts the raw materials to pursue equity-inducing personnel practices. The ultimate impact of their movement on sports as well as the broader society remains unknown. What is clear, however, is that in challenging the mighty NFL, this small group shook presumptions long informing head coach hiring and pioneered an extraordinary, and heretofore untold, civil rights story.

1

BALTIMORE LOVE

"WE WERE ROOTING FOR YOU TODAY."

They were the last words Tony Dungy expected to hear from the bus drivers charged with transporting his team to the airport. His Indianapolis Colts had just walked confidently into M&T Bank Stadium in Baltimore, Maryland, and defeated the hometown Ravens 15–6 to advance to the 2006 NFL season's AFC Championship Game. Ravens fans had every reason to be sour and seemingly no reason to support the opponents' victorious head coach. The Ravens had posted thirteen regular-season wins and only three losses, and they were favored to beat the Colts. From the very beginning, however, the Ravens' attack proved ineffective against Indy's swarming defense. In sixty minutes of football, the Ravens mustered only two field goals and saw their Super Bowl dreams wither. For Baltimoreans, the loss was painful. That the Colts inflicted the loss made it nearly unbearable.

The Indianapolis Colts had once been the Baltimore Colts, after all, and during the team's thirty-year tenure in Baltimore, the Colts proudly represented the people. They were a hard-nosed team in a hardscrabble town. There were certainly years when the Colts did not perform up to expectations and fans responded with lackluster attendance, but the team and the town generally had a wonderful marriage.

Then, on a snowy late March night in 1984, it was over. As the city slept, a fleet of Mayflower moving trucks and a small army of movers entered the Colts' training complex, packed up the Colts' belongings, and carried them off to Indiana. Fans who had excitedly debated the team's prospects the night before had no team in the morning.

It was devastating, and the fans attacked. They mourned their loss by peppering the team owner, Robert Irsay, with a barrage of hate mail, threats, and derision. Not even Irsay's death in 1997, thirteen years after the move, protected him from their ire. Although the city by then had the Ravens, T-shirts depicting a Baltimorean urinating on Irsay's grave adorned many a chest when the Indianapolis Colts visited Baltimore to play.

The irony, of course, is that Irsay liked Baltimore. He had simply grown weary of old Memorial Stadium, the charming but outdated playing facility his Colts shared with Major League Baseball's Baltimore Orioles. Irsay had tried desperately to convince the city that the Colts needed a newer facility, but negotiations over a new stadium stalled and relations deteriorated. Fearing a disgruntled and increasingly erratic Irsay would take his team elsewhere, Baltimore launched a preemptive strike. Under heavy lobbying from the city, the Maryland legislature began working to authorize Baltimore to expropriate the Colts by way of eminent domain, and on March 27, 1984, one of the state's two legislative bodies passed the authorizing bill. The next day, before the second body could act, Irsay skipped town with his team. Whatever the details precipitating Irsay's midnight move, Baltimoreans never forgave Irsay or his franchise, and twenty-two years later, when Dungy's Colts visited Baltimore for the first-ever Colts-Ravens playoff game, the tension was palpable.

Dungy generally began game days with a leisurely stroll alongside one of his assistant coaches. On this day, though, he questioned the wisdom of this pregame ritual. One thing he did not need before such a crucial game was a confrontation with angry fans harboring old grudges. Dungy ultimately decided to take the walk and was relieved to find that the people he met along his way were gracious and friendly. But the experience proved to be the calm before a storm that descended hours later as the Colts' team buses labored toward the stadium.

Never in Dungy's career had he received such a vitriolic reception. Neither the notoriously surly New York Giants fans nor the Philadelphia Eagles supporters, the latter famous for once pelting Santa Claus with snowballs, had anything on these maniacs. They were, as Dungy later recollected, simply "vicious." And that was *before* the Colts eliminated their team from the playoffs.

Dungy certainly did not expect from the bus drivers the sort of bile the purple-and-black-clad battalion of Ravens fans had spewed, but he was understandably surprised to learn they were pleased with the game's outcome. "Even though we live in Baltimore," one explained, speaking for the rest, "we want you to win and get to the Super Bowl."

Once Dungy heard them out, he knew why they'd said what they did. The bus drivers were African American, and they were proud of him.

The prospect of an African American head coach reaching the Super Bowl was remarkable because, for the bulk of the NFL's existence, simply attaining a head coaching position was virtually impossible for an African American. Indeed, when Dungy entered the NFL's coaching ranks in 1981 as an assistant coach with the Pittsburgh Steelers, the NFL featured no African American head coaches. Fifteen years later, in 1996, after distinguishing himself on the coaching staffs of the Steelers, the Kansas City Chiefs, and the Minnesota Vikings, Dungy received his first NFL head coaching offer. He accepted and promptly inherited the League's most hapless team, the Tampa Bay Buccaneers. When Dungy became the Buccaneers' head coach, the team had compiled only three winning seasons in franchise history and had not qualified for the play-offs since 1982. Dungy promised to turn the team around, and in short order he did.

During Dungy's second season at the helm, the Buccaneers won ten games against only six losses, qualified for the playoffs, and won their first playoff game before bowing out to the defending Super Bowl champion Green Bay Packers. Two years later, the Buccaneers won their division and narrowly missed a Super Bowl appearance when they lost a nail-biter to the St. Louis Rams in the NFC Championship game. Amazingly, after another two years, both of which featured playoff appearances, Dungy was fired.

The termination shook Dungy. He firmly believed he had done things the right way. He'd resurrected a moribund franchise and made winning in Tampa Bay an expectation rather than an aberration, and he did so with integrity and class, never cursing and rarely raising his voice. Dungy was no softy, to be sure. Football is a brutal sport and Dungy had spent most of his life playing and coaching it. Moreover, his specialty as a coach was constructing and coaching hard-hitting and dominant defenses. To do so effectively, as Dungy had for years, requires a hard edge. Dungy certainly cultivated toughness, but he did not permit intentionally injurious play and ultimately insisted that his players aspire to be good men as well as good athletes. He had done his best with the Buccaneers, but evidently it was not enough.

As Dungy packed his belongings and moved out of his office at the Bucs' training facility on a cold Tampa Bay night in January 2002, the damp, rainy weather reflected his disposition. He was not alone in his discontent. Many commentators, football insiders, and fans found the firing absurd. They believed Dungy had done the impossible in Tampa Bay by molding the Buccaneers into a consistent playoff contender, and some privately cried foul, insisting the Buccaneers would not have fired a white coach under the same circumstances.

Although disappointed, Dungy was undeterred, and when the Colts hired him as their head coach later in 2002 he quickly began improving his new team as he had improved the Buccaneers. In the years that followed, the Colts became a perennial championship contender, and the 2006 season, during which the Colts posted a 12–4 regular season record, was no different in that regard. The 2006 season was unique, though, in another respect: it featured a record seven African American head coaches, two of whom joined Dungy in the playoffs, each with a legitimate chance at Super Bowl glory.

Lovie Smith's Chicago Bears were even more impressive than Dungy's Colts during the regular season, posting a 13–3 record and earning the NFC's top playoff seed. And Herman Edwards' Kansas City Chiefs, although not as highly touted as the Colts or Bears, finished the regular season with a respectable 9–7 record and were playing inspired football as they entered the playoffs.

These three coaches—Dungy, Smith, and Edwards—were rivals, but they were also close friends. Both Smith and Edwards had worked under Dungy in Tampa Bay, and they were bound not just by mutual admiration and respect but also by a common struggle. Each had played football when an African American leading an NFL team as its head coach was, with the exception of Pollard's brief tenure a half century earlier, unprecedented. In addition, each had worked for years in coaching's lower echelons when the prospects of obtaining an NFL head coaching position were frighteningly slim no matter how valiantly or successfully they performed.

But that was the past, and as head coaches, they took pride in each other's successes. It was unavoidable, though, that one would be responsible for ending another's postseason, as Dungy's Colts and Edwards' Chiefs were scheduled to collide in Indianapolis in the first round of the playoffs. Before the game, while each man's Super Bowl hopes were still alive, they met to break bread. Smith, whose Bears received a first-round bye because of their number one NFC seed, drove down from Chicago to Indianapolis on the eve of the game and the three enjoyed a pleasant dinner.

The sense that this NFL season portended something truly special had been percolating for much of the year, and as the postseason began, that sense was not lost on the three friends. Chances were strong that one of them could, in a few weeks, be the first African

American head coach to win a Super Bowl. They all believed that Smith's Bears, with home-field advantage throughout the playoffs, would face the least resistance in reaching the Super Bowl but that the winner of the next day's game might well join Smith and his team on football's grandest stage.

Less than twenty-four hours later, Dungy's Colts held the Chiefs' star running back, Larry Johnson, to only thirty-two yards on thirteen carries en route to a dominating 23–8 victory, and a week after that, a Baltimorean who cheered for Dungy to beat the hometown Ravens was happily driving him out of an M&T Bank Stadium parking lot. The next day Smith would have his chance to move within a game of the Super Bowl, and Dungy would be watching with excitement.

These were bright times for Tony Dungy, as bright as his termination four years earlier was dark. Had it not been for his termination—or, more precisely, the way his termination impacted Mehri—the possibility of facing his friend and mentee in the Super Bowl might never have materialized. Indeed, Smith might never have ascended to a head coaching position at all. The same might well have been the case for many of the League's other African American head coaches. When Dungy left Tampa Bay, race was reliably predictive of success in attaining an NFL head coaching position. That all began to change on Dungy's first day of post-Buccaneers unemployment, when Mehri read about what transpired in Tampa, grew disgusted, and began to craft a strategy that would revolutionize the NFL.

2

AN IDEA'S ORIGIN

Were he still living, Martin Luther King Jr. would have been seventy-three years old on January 15, 2002. But he was, of course, gunned down nearly thirty-four years earlier as he pursued his dream of nationwide racial justice and equality.

Whether America had achieved the dream King articulated so gracefully from the Lincoln Memorial's steps several years before his 1968 assassination was debatable, and every year on his birthday commentators of all stripes explored the question. To Mehri, the answer was obvious: racial bias was alive and thriving. He'd built an entire legal practice on trying to defeat it.

Mehri acknowledged that the overt racial discrimination of King's day had largely receded, but he believed it had given way to a more subtle, often covert, sometimes subconscious form of discrimination that infected America more deeply than most people knew or were willing to admit. Mehri targeted this "second-generation" discrimination in the workplace, where he believed it ran rampant, through representing employees in racial discrimination suits against their employers.

Mehri respected King not only for his courage and his message but also for the legal developments his work spurred. Over the span of just a few years during America's turbulent civil rights era, in response to King's and others' enduring insistence that America embody its promise as a free democracy, the United States Congress revolutionized the nation's legal landscape with the Civil Rights Act of 1964, the Voting Rights Act of 1965, and the Fair Housing Act of 1968. Each of the three statutes augmented the nation's body of laws with prohibitions against discrimination, but Mehri was partial to the Civil Rights Act, and particularly to the seventh of the statute's eleven titles. After all, Title VII, which prohibits employers from terminating, refusing to hire, or otherwise discriminating based on a person's race, color, religion, sex, or national origin, made his employment discrimination practice possible. Mehri litigated with the tools King helped create, and he felt deeply indebted.

On this particular anniversary of King's birth, however, Mehri had no celebratory plans. He began the morning as he began every morning, sorting through the *Washington Post*, pulling out the sports section, and scouring it for NFL news. He would return to the other sections later, eventually reading the business news, and then turning to the latest developments in national politics. But the NFL was always first. It was his refuge.

Family and work aside, nothing mattered more to Mehri than football. One would not suspect that, though, by looking at him. Mehri was of average height, slightly built, and bespectacled. He impressed neither as an athlete nor as having the capacity to so enjoy such an aggressive and sometimes brutal sport. Yet he loved the game with a passion and had since childhood.

How precisely that love developed is a bit of a mystery, even to Mehri. He certainly did not inherit it from his parents, both of whom immigrated to the United States from Iran before Mehri's birth, and neither of whom, to Mehri's knowledge, ever exhibited interest in football or any other sport.

To them, education was paramount. The Iranian government had terminated Bahijeh Mehri's university education and barred her from leaving the country when her roommate reported she was speaking critically of the shah, but Parviz Mehri's medical education provided him the status necessary to persuade Iranian officials to permit his young wife's passage out of Iran and the financial means to effectuate it. Mehri's parents knew there was nothing more important they could bestow on their firstborn child than education, and they believed sports were unavoidably a distraction. By any measure, the single-minded educational focus worked. After attending Hartwick College in Oneonta, New York, Mehri attended and graduated from Cornell Law School.

Athletically, Mehri was far less accomplished. Although he played as much pickup touch football as possible as a child, he competed in only one season of organized play during his formative years— Pop Warner football as a thirteen-year-old. He signed up to play against his parents' wishes, played the season with their grudging support, and never signed up again. Still, Mehri's brief gridiron experience invigorated his love for football, and he channeled that love into fandom. He became a devoted and knowledgeable football fan and most enjoyed watching the game played at its highest level, in the NFL.

Although Mehri lived in Connecticut, he adopted the Dallas Cowboys as his favorite team. The Cowboys, dubbed "America's Team," were the League's glamour franchise. The large blue five-pointed star adorning the players' silver helmets had become iconic, as had the Cowboys' cheerleaders—the first in the League to don revealing uniforms and dance as much as cheer. The team's mystique, together with its winning ways, attracted countless football fans who otherwise would have supported their respective local teams, and Mehri was among them. But the Cowboys appealed to Mehri for an additional reason. He admired their head coach, Tom Landry, for his approach to his job and the results it bore. During the twenty-nine years Landry stalked the Cowboys' sidelines and evolved into one of the game's great coaches, he rarely screamed or gesticulated aggressively; rather, he spoke quietly and maintained his composure. Landry's sideline manner impressed Mehri, and when Mehri later practiced law, a profession given to histrionics and grandstanding in some quarters, he tried to do so with poise. He sometimes failed in that regard, and when he did, he quickly scrambled to gather himself. Angry rants, he'd learned, generally yielded poor outcomes.

Tony Dungy reminded Mehri of Landry and, to some extent, of himself. Dungy too approached his job with calm determination and achieved success. Although Mehri would never abandon the Cowboys, he appreciated what Dungy had done with the Buccaneers and the way in which he had done it.

So when Mehri turned to the *Post*'s sports page that January morning and read the succinct headline "Dungy Out," he was floored. Mehri found the termination incomprehensible. Dungy had led the Buccaneers to more success than the franchise had ever experienced, and the team was still winning. As Mehri read the article under the headline, sadness gave way to anger. He'd felt the same way two weeks earlier when the Minnesota Vikings fired their head coach, Dennis Green.

Green, an African American, sparkled during his ten years with the Vikings. Under his leadership, the team won a remarkable 63 percent of its games and, in one year, won fifteen of its sixteen regular-season games. More impressive still, Green led his team to eight playoff appearances and two conference championship games. Nevertheless, after Green's first losing season—a season doomed from the start by the tragic death of one of the team's best offensive linemen—the Vikings fired him.

Mehri viewed both firings as patently unjust, and in light of his familiarity with workplace discrimination and the instincts he had developed through fighting it day after day, he deemed them racially driven. Having followed the NFL since the early 1970s, Mehri was well familiar with the long-standing racial homogeneity in the League's head coaching ranks. For years commentators had lamented the lack of diversity among NFL head coaches and called for change. And to the

NFL's credit, it had attempted to improve on that front through various programs over the years.

Still, the League's teams rarely hired African American head coaches, and it seemed to Mehri that the inequitable treatment prevailed not only at the hiring stage but, for those few who attained head coaching positions, also at the firing stage.

First, there was Shell's experience. In Shell's first full season as the Raiders' head coach, he transformed the struggling team's fortunes, leading the Raiders to twelve regular-season wins and then to a berth in the AFC championship game. All told, over the course of his five-plus years in charge, Shell won fifty-four games while losing only thirty-eight, and he posted winning records in all but one season. In 1994, however, on the heels of two consecutive winning seasons, Raiders owner Al Davis fired him. Although it would take Davis twelve years to finally admit Shell's firing was undeserved, Mehri recognized the injustice immediately. Green's firing seemed even more preposterous, in light of both his sustained success over a decade's course and his team's preseason tragedy in his terminal year.

In Mehri's view, Dungy's firing surpassed the other two in sheer absurdity, particularly when viewed in the context of the Buccaneers' previous head coach firings. As Mehri would later explain, "Before Dungy, Sam Wyche coached the Buccaneers for four losing seasons before being fired. Before Wyche, Richard Williamson coached the Buccaneers for two losing seasons before being fired. Before Williamson, Ray Perkins coached the Buccaneers for four losing seasons before being fired." Dungy, in contrast, coached the Buccaneers for five straight nonlosing seasons, established a tradition of excellence, and was fired.

The double standard Dungy faced could not have been more glaring. The Buccaneers fired Dungy's predecessors, all white, for losing. They fired Dungy even though he won. Although Dungy had not captured the League's ultimate prize, a Super Bowl championship, surely he merited more time at the helm.

After reading of Green's dismissal, Mehri had stewed for a few hours, then put the matter behind him and returned to his work. But

Dungy's termination was the last straw, and at his kitchen table, on King's seventy-third birthday, with the *Post*'s sports page lying in front of him, he decided the NFL had to change.

To effectuate change, Mehri knew, he had to convincingly prove, even to skeptics, that the competition for NFL head coaching positions was fundamentally unfair and that African American coaches were judged against more exacting standards than their white colleagues. Mehri believed the trend of head coach hirings and firings throughout the League over the preceding several years supported his hypothesis, but he knew anecdotes could propel his argument only so far. Cynics would trot out counteranecdotes and attribute seeming disparities to coincidence.

They might, for example, point to the Buccaneers' early playoff exits in 2000 and 2001 as just cause for terminating Dungy or argue that Dungy's seemingly mellow demeanor was inadequate to motivate football players for their most intense games. Others might challenge accounts of African American head coaching success generally with an account of Ray Rhodes' NFL head coaching career. They would grant that Rhodes excelled in his first two seasons with the Philadelphia Eagles in 1995 and 1996, but note that he followed those years with two years in which the Eagles lost a combined twenty-two games, won only nine, and went winless in the team's sixteen matches on the road. Despite Rhodes' struggles, they would point out, the Green Bay Packers gave him a head coaching job the following year.

So that morning, aware that a war of anecdotes would do little more than provide momentary fodder for sports talk radio debates and then quietly recede from the public consciousness, Mehri resolved to engage the issue on a different ground, a ground on which equal opportunity battles in professional sports had not previously been waged. He would seek to prove racial discrimination by way of statistical analysis.

Although not a statistician, Mehri felt comfortable with statistics, and he had been wielding them on his clients' behalf for years. As an employment discrimination class action lawyer, he had no other choice. Without statistical support, plaintiffs who band together as a class to sue their employers are generally doomed. Whatever the facts of their cases, to achieve success they must make a statistically significant discrimination showing. That is to say, they must, using statistics, show that discrimination rather than coincidence explains the adverse employment actions they suffered.

Here, though, there was no class and no suit. But Mehri believed if the statistics revealed what he hoped they would, both were possible. And because both would be possible, he believed neither would be necessary. He believed if he confronted the NFL with proof that some of its member clubs treated head coaches differently based on color, the NFL would have little choice but to address the situation.

The prospect excited Mehri, but he knew the project would have to wait. Just two months earlier he had filed suit against Johnson & Johnson on behalf of African American and Latino employees alleging various forms of employment discrimination, and the new case had stretched his firm of seven lawyers to capacity. In any event, Mehri was not sure he wanted to tackle America's most profitable and popular professional sports league alone. Before moving forward, he wanted to get Johnnie Cochran on board.

MEHRI AND COCHRAN could just as easily have become enemies as friends when their paths first crossed in 2000. In fact, were Mehri a more reactionary lawyer, he might have viewed Cochran as attempting to steal his clients and torpedo what was then the most important case of his career, his class action lawsuit against the Coca-Cola Company.

When Mehri filed suit against Coke, he risked everything. Several months before filing, he had turned down a partnership offer from the Washington, D.C., law firm of Cohen, Milstein, Hausfeld & Toll, where he'd litigated for more than eight years. Cohen Milstein had given Mehri his start and had introduced him to class action work, for which he was grateful, but the firm was large and diversified, with a hand in various practice areas ranging from antitrust to securities. Cohen Milstein offered breadth, but Mehri sought to focus his talents on civil rights lawyering and did not believe he would be able to do that as a Cohen Milstein junior partner.

So Mehri walked away from partnership and decided instead to branch out on his own. Despite having no clients and little capital, he knew that if he wanted to found his own firm, he had to do it then. He was young yet, only thirty-five years old, and thus had time to recover if his new venture flopped.

In addition, he was riding a publicity wave of the sort attorneys rarely enjoy. He had just led a team of Cohen Milstein lawyers in a three-year-long class action employment discrimination lawsuit against Texaco that yielded an unprecedented settlement for the African American employees the firm represented. Texaco, knowing it was outmatched and unable to refute claims of rampant organization-wide racial discrimination, agreed to institute an array of systematic initiatives designed to thwart future discrimination, and to pay plaintiffs $176 million in damages. Mehri was merely an associate at the firm, but he brought the case in the door, nurtured client relationships, and determined the strategy that ultimately spawned victory. Whomever the firm's internal case management files named as the partner in charge, everyone knew it was Mehri's case, and when it was over, everyone knew it was Mehri's win.

The Texaco case made Mehri a star in the class action litigation world, which meant grudging respect from defense lawyers and referrals from other plaintiffs' lawyers and friends. Mehri didn't know if he would ever again be as well situated to launch his own practice, and he seized the moment.

The timing was perfect. Before Mehri was able to furnish his modest new office space and hire a suitable staff, Linda Ingram, an employee at Coke in Atlanta, called him for help, complaining that she was being discriminatorily compensated. Ingram's story intrigued Mehri, but he needed more information, and once he was able to hire an associate and a paralegal, he traveled to Atlanta to meet Ingram in person. Ingram had by then organized dozens of other African Americans who told similar stories. Mehri decided to take the case, and he began to accrue a formidable collection of damning affidavits.

Mehri did not know the true strength of his clients' claims until a mysterious package materialized on his office doorstep shortly after he returned from Atlanta. The package was small, just a few inches thick, and bore no identifying marks. Mehri tore away the outer packaging to reveal a stack of documents, which, like the envelope in which they'd come, betrayed no trace of authorship. Their origin, however, was clear. They came from someone at Coke who wanted him to win. Mehri had before him page after page of Coca-Cola employee salary information, which under analysis revealed massive racially driven disparities.

Mehri was certain the documents proved that Coke was violating Title VII, but even with such evidence he knew that successfully suing Coke in Atlanta would be extremely difficult, because Coke essentially owned the city. As the world's largest beverage company and one of the city's premier economic engines, the soft drink giant wielded untold power throughout Atlanta. Coke executives had served as city officials and civic leaders in Atlanta for generations, and it seemed every Atlantan had ties of some sort to the Coca-Cola empire.

Mehri knew he would need more resources than he and his skeletal staff could muster, but securing co-counsel to assist them proved challenging. Firm after firm, citing the case's likely futility, rejected his invitation. The refrain was simple and consistent: "Suing Coke in Atlanta is like suing the Pope in the Vatican. You can't win."

At long last Mehri convinced a respected Atlanta-based law firm, Bondurant, Mixson & Elmore, to sign on to the case with him. And for two grueling years, with Bondurant Mixson's assistance, Mehri fought Coke with a singular focus and a fair measure of desperation. He had funneled all of his firm's resources into the case, and if he failed, the firm would implode. But by June 2000, failure was the furthest thing from Mehri's mind. The litigation had overcome numerous obstacles, and Mehri and his co-counsel were on the verge of brokering a historic settlement with Coke.

Then Johnnie Cochran appeared.

Just as the parties were preparing to settle, Mehri learned that several of his clients, on whose behalf he had toiled for two years, wanted to sue Coke separately, and Cochran, it seemed, was one of their lawyers. The other was Willie Gary, a talented and flamboyant Florida-based trial attorney who had amassed a fortune litigating suits of all sorts and whose promotional materials featured him shadowboxing to the *Rocky* theme song.

Since the case's inception, Gary had been trying to involve himself. Initially, not long after Mehri filed the suit, Gary approached Coke in hopes of representing the company as defense counsel. Later, once Coke opted against retaining him, he turned his attention to the plaintiffs' side, reportedly promising class members "he would get them more money than Mehri ever could." Although Coke spent $5 million a year advertising on a cable station in which Gary held an ownership stake, creating a seeming conflict of interest, four of Mehri's eight class representatives defected.

At that point, Gary contacted Mehri and Bondurant Mixson and requested to be co-counsel. When they refused, Gary filed a separate suit, which, at least according to the defectors' complaint, Cochran co-signed.

Everything looked to be unraveling. Mehri had no way of knowing whether other class members would abandon him for Gary and the world-renowned Cochran or if the new action would frighten Coke away from the settlement he had worked so hard to broker. Mehri and his co-counsel were furious. They viewed the developments as wildly unethical and quickly resolved to file a motion with the court protesting the conduct. The only question was whom they would implicate in the motion, and the answer was clear to everyone but Mehri. Gary and Cochran were listed together on the new complaint as counsel of record, so it made sense to aim fire at both. Still, Mehri urged caution. They didn't trust Gary, but this was the first they had heard from Cochran. Mehri argued that since Cochran had not yet shown himself to be a bad actor in the context of the case, they should limit their allegations of wrongdoing to Gary and simply send Cochran a copy of the motion. After some convincing, the team agreed. It would prove to be among the best decisions of Mehri's career.

Cochran was at a retreat in Jamaica when his office received the copy of the motion, and as soon as he learned of it, he called Mehri. Cochran acknowledged that he had worked with Gary on previous matters, but he told Mehri he had never agreed to represent plaintiffs against Coke and was not sure how his name had materialized on the complaint. Pleased that Mehri had not implicated him in the developing Coke controversy, Cochran, upon returning from his retreat, invited Mehri to his New York offices so the two could meet in person. Mehri and Cochran thereafter became fast friends and soon began exploring collaborative possibilities. Mehri was ultimately able to settle with Coke for $192.5 million, and when he moved on to other cases he often solicited Cochran's assistance.

When Mehri experienced his Martin Luther King Jr. Day brainstorm, therefore, turning to Cochran was natural. Although Mehri knew that the fear Cochran inspired among opponents might come in handy if the project evolved into a battle with the NFL, that is not what compelled Mehri to seek Cochran's involvement. Mehri approached Cochran with the project because the time the two had been spending together convinced Mehri that Cochran was not the slick-lawyering celebrity hound most of America seemingly perceived him to be but rather was at base a civil rights lawyer. And Mehri was right. Cochran was a product of the African American struggle, and although few in the public space seemed to acknowledge it, he had decades earlier committed himself to ensuring a less onerous struggle for black America's future generations.

Cochran's great-grandparents were born into slavery. Although they lived to experience emancipation, they also lived to recognize, as did their contemporaries, that emancipation was not the same as freedom. Racial terror and profound economic oppression, it turned out, would indefinitely extend African American subordination in spite of the Thirteenth Amendment's promise that slavery was no more.

Chief among the new forms of race-based oppression was the institution of sharecropping, in which landowners rented to tenants plots of land to farm and advanced the tenants money for seed and tools, and then, after harvest, provided the tenants a share of the proceeds. The share was minimal, of course, and generally insufficient or scarcely sufficient to repay the advances, thus producing spiraling debt or, at best, stagnant poverty, which left the tenants little choice but to continue sharecropping year after year. This cycle, which spawned persistent economic dependence and, in essence, indefinite servitude, snared Cochran's grandparents.

Alonzo Cochran and his wife, Hannah, spent much of their working lives sharecropping in Caddo Parish, Louisiana. Although they generally managed to finish the season with a minor profit, the landowners from whom they rented, the Hutchinsons, paid them in coupons redeemable only at the Hutchinsons' store, requiring that the Cochrans return that profit to the Hutchinsons in exchange for goods. Alonzo sharecropped until he died in 1935 when doctors attempted to repair his bleeding ulcer but instead bungled the surgery. The doctors admitted their mistake, but as Cochran would later remark in his memoir, for an African American patient treated by white doctors "in Louisiana, in 1935, mistakes were of no consequence." There would be no remedy. Prevailing racial dynamics simply would not allow it.

Before his death, however, Alonzo invested all he had in his only child, Johnnie L. Cochran Sr. With whatever money Alonzo was able to save as he tended the Hutchinsons' land, he bought books for his son and constantly implored him to strive for academic excellence. "I never had a chance," Alonzo frequently exhorted, "so I want you to make an impression wherever you go, on every level." Johnnie shone academically, ultimately moving as a young teen to Shreveport to live with his aunt and attend schools with more to offer than those in Caddo Parish.

Alonzo's deepest wish was that his son go to college, so it would have devastated him to know that his death, or rather the inequitable circumstances surrounding his life at the time of his death, would derail Johnnie's postsecondary education plans. Alonzo happened to die with crops in the ground, which meant he had incurred the debt necessary to plant but had not yet harvested the crops he would need to discharge that debt under his sharecropping arrangement with the Hutchinsons. So Johnnie, who had graduated at the top of his high school class, had to postpone college and return to Caddo Parish to bring in his father's crop. After picking hundreds of pounds of cotton per day that autumn, Johnnie repaid the Hutchinsons, but with his father gone and nobody to support his mother, Johnnie moved with her back to Shreveport and joined the workforce as a Walgreen's drugstore delivery boy. He would never have the chance to attend college.

His son, Johnnie L. Cochran Jr., however, would. Inspired by his father's zest for academic achievement, Cochran excelled through school. As he did so, he began to narrow his academic focus, and on May 17, 1954, when Cochran was sixteen years old, he crystallized his ambition. On that day the United States Supreme Court issued its decision in *Brown v. Board of Education of Topeka, Kansas*, proclaiming the long-standing segregationist "separate but equal" educational philosophy to be fatally flawed. "Separate educational facilities," the court reasoned, were "inherently *unequal*," and segregated public education was, therefore, unconstitutional.

It was among the greatest days of Cochran's life. He reveled in the decision and its implications for the country, and he idolized Thurgood Marshall, the young lawyer who argued the case and who eventually would become the nation's first African American Supreme Court justice. Cochran decided then that he wanted to use the law to spur societal change. He attended the University of California at Los Angeles, from which he earned his bachelor's degree, and he shortly thereafter earned his law degree from Loyola Marymount University School of Law.

As Cochran became increasingly familiar with the legal system, first as a prosecutor in the Los Angeles City Attorney's Office and then as a private practitioner, he developed a fierce dedication to the Constitution's principles as well as an enduring belief that African Americans were too often denied its protections. Cochran accepted cases of all sorts—civil as well as criminal—and represented clients of all races, but he took special pride in protecting African Americans from a legal system he viewed as stacked against them.

As Cochran's reputation for brilliant lawyering burgeoned, so too did his roster of clients and his wealth. Celebrities began seeking Cochran's assistance, and as their lawyer, he in turn became a celebrity. He loved trying cases and he loved growing his practice. So when former NFL star O. J. Simpson, charged with murdering his former wife in 1994, sought Cochran's representation, Cochran accepted the challenge, embraced his role as Simpson's lawyer, and won the case.

The victory would forever alter Cochran's life. Simpson was African American, his ex-wife Nicole was white, and racial issues predictably infused the case. Cochran certainly did not shy away from race in defending Simpson. Rather, he seized upon it, revealing one of the investigating officers, Mark Fuhrman, as a racist and contextualizing the case within the nation's racial dynamic. Indeed, Cochran's closing argument began in earnest not with a discussion of the evidence or a bold statement of his client's innocence but with a reference to Frederick Douglass, the abolitionist and civil rights leader. Countless Americans, including many lawyers, viewed Cochran's defense as divisive and unethical and accused him of inappropriately playing the "race card" for his client's benefit. Others, noting that the prosecution had introduced Fuhrman into the case as a witness, argued Cochran merely "responded to the cards he was dealt" and would have neglected his duty of zealous representation had he not attacked Fuhrman's credibility on racial grounds and otherwise explored the case's racial underpinnings. Still, Cochran's detractors constituted the majority view, and upon Simpson's acquittal, Cochran and his family were bombarded with racially inflamed hate mail and death threats.

None of the writers seemed to acknowledge that three years before accepting Simpson's case, Cochran represented truck driver Reginald Denny, a white man famously attacked in the street when Los Angeles exploded following acquittals in the cases of four police officers who savaged African American motorist Rodney King after a 1991 traffic stop. After the verdict in the king case, Denny happened to be driving a truckload of sand to a construction site in the Inglewood section of town when several African American men pulled him from the vehicle and nearly beat him to death with their hands, their feet, and a concrete block. Community members asked Cochran to represent two of the defendants, but he declined, choosing instead to bring civil charges on Denny's behalf. If those who sent the O. J. Simpson–related hate mail knew about Cochran's choices in the Denny matter, they conveniently disregarded them in calling for his head.

Not all of the mail Cochran received after Simpson's acquittal was negative. He received some accolades as well. Scores of people loved him, and scores of others hated him, but to them all, he was O.J.'s lawyer. The trial had seemingly rendered trivial all of the other work Cochran had done as an attorney, which made him uncomfortable. He certainly was pleased with his victory and quite enjoyed the substantial media exposure and fame it earned him, but he did not want it to entirely define his practice. His body of work was much broader. Indeed, before and after the O.J. case, he was Geronimo Pratt's lawyer, and in his view, if any case defined his practice, it was Pratt's.

In 1972 Cochran defended Pratt, a young, poor African American man unjustly accused of murder because of his affiliation with the Black Panther Party. Cochran lost the trial and Pratt was convicted. From that day forward, Cochran worked free of charge to secure Pratt's freedom, and twenty-seven years later, in light of substantial evidence that Pratt was framed for the murder, the conviction was overturned and Pratt was freed. Cochran believed the Pratt representation—the commitment to assist the underresourced, the intolerance for injustice, the dogged persistence—best characterized him as a lawyer. It was the representation of which he always seemed most proud.

Whatever the public perception, Cochran was committed to civil rights advocacy, and when Mehri approached him with a concern about inequitable opportunities for NFL coaches of color, but with no client and thus no real possibility of remuneration for either man's time, Cochran enthusiastically agreed to help.

It didn't hurt that Cochran loved sports and that he loved football above all others. He was a former high school quarterback and a die-hard Oakland Raiders supporter. Beyond enjoying the game, however, Cochran understood sports' import to society. He recognized that racial progress in the sports world often helped propel broader societal progress.

As a child, Cochran and his father re-created Joe Louis' punches as the family's radio brought the action of the Brown Bomber's fights, blow by blow, into their living room. Cochran loved Louis not just for his pugilistic dominance but also for the grace he displayed and the admiration and respect he commanded from Americans of all hues. The young Cochran was similarly enamored of Jackie Robinson. He cheered Robinson's Brooklyn Dodgers for breaking baseball's color barrier and jeered the team's opponents for their segregationist fervor. Even as a child, he believed the games Robinson played were not merely athletic contests. They were social statements.

Mehri and Cochran both knew that forcing the NFL to come to terms with its dearth of African American head coaches would be a social statement as well. Millions of Americans spent their autumn Sundays glued to the television set watching NFL games and familiarizing themselves with their favorite team's players and coaches.

If Joe Louis' career and Jackie Robinson's career suggested progress, however slow and hard-fought it was, what did a few dozen white men leading thousands of mostly African American men into weekly physical competition suggest? What did it say about the country? More importantly, what did it say *to* the country? What were viewers to deduce—that whites had brains and African Americans had brawn, that whites were natural leaders in a way African Americans were not?

Mehri and Cochran knew too many had worked too hard and for too long in trying to dismantle the age-old stereotype of the intellectually inferior African American to see it subtly reinforced every Sunday. They also knew that defeating the stereotype on NFL Sundays could, like other sports-related antidiscrimination victories throughout American history, have meaningful societal implications.

The matter of statistics remained, however, and while both lawyers recognized their importance to the project, neither had sufficient expertise to conduct the necessary analysis. They would need to involve a third party. When Mehri had commissioned statistical analyses in previous cases, he'd often turned to University of Pennsylvania economics professor Janice Madden. He trusted her work and her discretion, and so solicited her to confidentially run the numbers he needed to make his case against the NFL. Mehri asked Madden to compare the coaching performances of African American head coaches and white head coaches over the preceding fifteen years, and then he nervously waited. Without statistically significant analytical support for their proposition that racial discrimination was impeding African American coaches' careers in the NFL, Mehri and Cochran knew their project would fizzle. If, on the other hand, the statistics supported their hypothesis, they liked their chances of profoundly changing the League. It all depended on the stats.

3

SUPERIOR PERFORMANCE, INFERIOR OPPORTUNITIES

"No matter how we look at success, black coaches are performing better. The data are consistent with blacks having to be better coaches than the whites in order to get a job as a head coach in the NFL."

Madden's conclusion was at the same time anticipated and shocking. As longtime football fans and students of the game, Mehri and Cochran had intuited what Madden's study now corroborated, but they were not entirely prepared to hear a nationally renowned economist confirm their suspicions. After Madden presented her analysis, however, the lawyers knew they were heavily armed to challenge the NFL. The numbers were even more striking than they had imagined.

African American head coaches bested their white counterparts in seemingly every measurable category. In their first season as head coach of a team, African Americans soundly outperformed white first-year head coaches, averaging 2.7 more wins over the sixteen-game regular season. In their seasons before being terminated, African American head coaches were again superior, averaging 1.3 more wins. Most important, throughout their tenures African American head coaches led their teams to an average of more than nine wins per season, while white coaches led their teams to eight wins per season. Although that one-game differential initially might seem marginal, it is anything but. In a sixteen-game season, one win is often the difference between a playoff berth and the season's end. Moreover, no win is more important than a team's ninth. During the fifteen years Madden studied, 60 percent of teams winning nine games made the playoffs, and fewer than 10 percent of teams winning eight games did the same.

Wondering whether these indications of African American head coaching superiority reflected African Americans being hired by stronger organizations with winning traditions, Madden assessed African American head coaches' records against those of the white head coaches who preceded and succeeded them with a particular team. This analysis revealed that African American head coaches inherited losing teams and turned them into winning teams; after they were fired, the teams got worse.

African Americans were, by the numbers, simply better head coaches, and it wasn't even close. The reason for their superiority was obvious to Mehri and Cochran, and it had nothing to do with melanin. Rather, team decision makers held African American head coaching candidates to higher standards than whites and tended to hire only those who incontrovertibly dwarfed their competition. Once hired, the African American coaches' superior experience and expertise showed on the sidelines, and they typically outcoached their opponents.

Mehri and Cochran were hardly alone in recognizing the double standard African American head coaching candidates faced. Sports columnists had occasionally detailed it in articles, noting that for decades African American assistant coaches with impeccable credentials and extraordinary success as offensive or defensive coordinators, such as Sherman Lewis, Marvin Lewis, Emmitt Thomas, and others, diligently discharged their duties without ever receiving meaningful head coaching interviews. In contrast, they argued, white coaches with lesser resumes, such as Marty Mornhinweg, whom the Detroit Lions hired in 2001, and Dave McGinnis, whom the Arizona Cardinals hired in 2000, seemed to routinely land head coaching positions.

Art Shell, the former Los Angeles Raiders head coach, faced a double standard of his own. Despite having achieved success during his five-plus years in charge, Shell was ignored as a head coaching candidate for years after the Raiders terminated him. Meanwhile, former NFL head coaches Joe Bugel, Bruce Coslet, and Mike Shanahan, none of whom had ever compiled a winning record as a head coach but all of whom were white, landed subsequent head coaching positions.

Madden's statistics provided Mehri and Cochran a solid base around which to wrap these anecdotal inequities, and together the stats and the stories presented a powerful indictment. Winning lawsuits are born of such foundations, and Mehri and Cochran had both successfully litigated cases with far less. Even so, filing suit seemed nearly inconceivable for the most fundamental of reasons: they had neither a plaintiff to represent nor a defendant to sue.

Madden's statistics, which were easily Mehri and Cochran's most compelling evidence, revealed League-wide inequities and would, at best, be only minimally relevant to a suit against an individual team. Logic therefore would suggest that Mehri and Cochran sue the League. Suing the League for its teams' equal employment opportunity failures would be tricky, however. Courts had held that the NFL was not one entity comprised of thirty-two teams but an umbrella organization that staged contests among autonomous football clubs but did not otherwise dominate their affairs. Holding the League accountable for team personnel decisions thus seemed a difficult prospect.

Still, a part of Mehri wanted to press the matter. In one of sports law's seminal cases, the Los Angeles Memorial Coliseum Commission charged that the NFL's operations violated the Sherman Antitrust Act, which reads, in relevant part, "[E]very contract, combination . . . or conspiracy, in restraint of trade or commerce . . . is declared to be illegal." In response, the NFL launched the single-entity defense, arguing that because it and its member teams constituted a single entity it was incapable of conspiracy under the statute. If Mehri filed suit, the NFL would be arguing the opposite: that it and its teams are separate entities, none of which controlled the others' personnel decisions. Mehri recognized, of course, that the NFL's single-entity antitrust argument did not necessarily preclude the League from asserting its teams' independence regarding personnel matters, but he relished the thought of forcing the NFL into that awkward posture.

Even assuming that Mehri could convince a court that the NFL was an appropriate defendant, finding a plaintiff would be next to impossible. Playing for or coaching a professional sports team is, all things considered, a great way to make a living, and those fortunate enough to land such jobs tend not to jeopardize them by engaging in bitter legal battles. While victory might mean a higher salary or a promotion, it might also mean eventual excommunication from one's team, and possibly from the broader sports industry, which on the whole does not take kindly to potentially embarrassing challenges. It might, in essence, mean being the next Tommy Harper, and nobody wanted that.

Harper played baseball in the major leagues from 1962 to 1976, exhibiting speed, skill, and durability. But his on-field talent did not shape his legacy. In the unwritten annals of African American sport, Harper was the man who challenged the storied Boston Red Sox with federal racial discrimination charges and lost his career.

After playing ten years in the majors, Harper joined the Red Sox in 1972 with high hopes. Although the Red Sox franchise, which had been Major League Baseball's longest holdout against integration, retained a racially discordant reputation, Harper did not anticipate what he encountered upon joining the team for spring training in Winter Haven, Florida. Preseason workouts had barely begun when Harper observed a curious phenomenon. Often, after practices, small cards mysteriously appeared in some players' lockers and not others. Harper knew neither what they signified nor who delivered them. He just knew he never received one. Perplexed, he queried one of his African American teammates, Reggie Smith.

"What are these?" asked Harper quizzically.

"Cards to get in the Elks Club."

"Where's ours?"

"We don't get one," Smith matter-of-factly answered.

Harper had happened upon the worst-kept secret in the Red Sox clubhouse. Every year during spring training, the Winter Haven Elks Club provided Red Sox personnel free meals and hospitality. The club excluded African Americans, however, and made no exception for ballplayers. The Red Sox supported the policy, routinely distributing the club's free passes, which were redeemable for hearty dinners, to only its white players' and coaches' lockers.

The Red Sox complicity in the Elks' discrimination irked Harper, and in 1973, after enduring the racist ritual for a second straight year, he vented, discussing the matter with African American *Boston Globe* reporter Larry Whiteside but asking that Whiteside not write about the discriminatory spring training tradition. Harper knew a public complaint would cost him his job, and he resolved to ignore the mistreatment.

After playing for several more years, some with other teams, Harper returned to Boston as a coach in 1980 only to find that the Elks still provided white team personnel free meals and that Red Sox management still abetted such discrimination. In almost a decade, nothing had changed.

Still, Harper endured the indignity without comment, hoping the following spring training would be different. But every year the ritual was repeated. Finally, in 1984, Harper broached the matter with Red Sox chief operating officer Haywood Sullivan, who assured him the Red Sox would cease the practice. The next year, though, the Sox once again distributed Elks passes to white players only, and Harper's patience expired. When the *Globe*'s Michael Madden approached Harper that spring and asked him about the Elks Club, Harper shared his experience. On the strength of Harper's comments, Madden investigated the story, and in March 1985 he broke it:

WINTER HAVEN, FLA.—Sitting on the bar of the Elks Club, dead center in the middle as if it had been measured, was a large glass container. Scrawled on its side was the hand-written plea to support the restorations of the Statue of Liberty, a noble cause for which "The Elks have pledged $1 million." The jar was half full with paper money of all denominations.

A middle-aged man with glasses and a florid face who gave his name as Bill Carter was sitting on a barstool directly in front of the Liberty container. Amid the chaos and shouts that had erupted, this man was explaining why no blacks from the Red Sox ever had been inside the Winter Haven Elks Lodge.

"Simple," he said. "Because we don't allow any niggers in here."

It took Harper thirteen years, but he had finally exposed the shameful relationship between the Red Sox and the segregated Elks Club and cleared his conscience. The Red Sox, in turn, would clear Harper's professional calendar.

The day before the article saw print, Harper predicted the Red Sox would fire him, and once it hit the newsstands, he knew he was right. "After the article," Harper later recalled, "I don't think I had two hellos from Lou [Gorman, the team's general manager]. When I walked into the clubhouse the next day, it was like night and day. It was like I had dropped a bomb or something." Harper instantly became an outcast within his own organization. Stripped of his duties and essentially ignored, he was a Red Sox employee in name only, and in December 1985, once baseball had ceded its seasonal place in the nation's sports pages to football, basketball, and hockey, the Red Sox quietly dismissed Harper with no explanation.

But Harper had no intention of slinking meekly away, and he responded in a manner almost unthinkable at the time for an African American sports professional: he brought legal action.

Before launching a Title VII claim in federal court, a complainant must file a charge of discrimination with the United States Equal Employment Opportunity Commission (EEOC), which is precisely what Harper did. He charged the Red Sox with racial discrimination as well as with retaliatory termination and detailed the team's decades-long relationship with the Elks Club, the discriminatory pass distribution, the failed promise to cease such distribution, and his post-article shunning. Moreover, Harper explained that once he completed the mandated EEOC process, he was prepared to sue the Red Sox in federal court.

He would not have to do so. In July 1986, the EEOC's Charles L. Looney issued the commission's determination, which vindicated Harper and condemned the organization. "But for the fact [Harper] privately and publicly protested [the Red Sox'] discriminatory practice of distributing guest passes of the Winter Haven Fla., Elks Club to Caucasian employees only," wrote Looney, "there is no reason to believe [Harper] would have been terminated." Looney went on to find that the Red Sox "perpetuated a working environment hostile to minorities," and he chastised the organization for consistently refusing, over the course of many years, to reform. Saddled with Looney's determination, the Red Sox negotiated a low six-figure settlement with Harper, thus avoiding an embarrassing trial.

Harper had prevailed, but in classic pyrrhic fashion: by the time Looney rendered his decision, Harper was out of baseball. After exposing the Red Sox' discriminatory spring training practice in December 1985, Harper might conceivably have signed on with a different MLB team sympathetic to his plight. After involving the law, though, he stood no chance. While the Red Sox surged toward a 1986 World Series appearance, Harper worked at an auto body shop on Boston's Brookline Avenue, a mere two hundred yards from Fenway Park, the Red Sox' stadium. From the shop's front door, he could clearly see the ballpark and hear the summer cheers.

Harper would eventually get back into baseball, and more than a decade later the Red Sox, under new management, would bring him back into the organization in a low-level position. But he did not feel fully accepted as a part of the team until 2006, more than twenty years after he went to the EEOC. Harper won his challenge, but he suffered mightily for it.

Harper was certainly not the first African American athlete to endure painful consequences after challenging racial injustice. As boxing's first African American world heavyweight champion, from 1908 to 1915, the audacious and often irreverent Jack Johnson endured constant racial harassment, but he challenged it at every turn, refusing to be cowed by white supremacist ideology. In return, for being an "uppity nigger" as much as for any particular legal infraction, American authorities criminally prosecuted Johnson and forced him out of the country.

More than a half century later, when Harper was a young major leaguer, African American sprinters Tommie Smith and John Carlos finished first and third in the 200-meter track final at the 1968 Summer Olympics in Mexico City. After receiving their medals, as the American national anthem blared, they raised black-gloved fists to protest the racial inequality and poverty African Americans suffered back home. Instantly they were pariahs. The United States Olympic Committee promptly expelled both men from the team and sent them back to the United States, where they endured decades of abuse.

Between Johnson's struggle and the sprinters' stand, and up through Harper's battle with the Red Sox, many African American sports professionals challenged racism in ways big and small, to their detriment. Few, however, turned to the law. Harper wielded the law and did so successfully, but his experience proved that even a successful legal challenge was no protection from racially driven career sabotage, and at the turn of the twenty-first century his story still loomed over professional sports. Even those unfamiliar with its details sensed its lesson: keep quiet and keep your job. Indeed, for more than two decades following Harper's EEOC charge, virtually nobody mounted a serious legal challenge against racial discrimination in the professional sports industry, and as Mehri and Cochran contemplated how best to utilize Madden's numbers, they had no reason to suspect anyone was prepared to do so.

Even on the off chance a prospective plaintiff emerged and a court found the NFL to be an appropriate defendant, battling the robustly resourced League was not appetizing. Large, wealthy defendants tend to beat back suits by slowing them down, filing motion after motion on often marginal issues in an attempt to sap plaintiffs' enthusiasm and drain their coffers. A full-blown suit against the NFL would likely devolve into a war of attrition, and if it did, Mehri and Cochran, who were pursuing the project pro bono, risked the legal equivalent of death by a thousand cuts.

All in all, working up a legal brief and challenging the NFL in court seemed a bad idea, but the information at their disposal made it ludicrous to do nothing. So Mehri and Cochran resolved to cobble their statistics and factoids into a report and release it to the public at a press conference. Previous experience working together had taught the lawyers that finding a mutually available date for a joint appearance would be challenging, and it was. Finally they scheduled September 30, 2002, to roll out the report.

Aside from being open on both men's calendars, the date had several benefits. Perhaps most important, it was only a few weeks into the NFL season. Head coaches likely would not be fired for months. Thus, if the report gained traction, it conceivably would be a factor once the annual head coaching carousel spun into motion. In addition, September 30 happened to be a Monday night, and the Ravens were hosting the Denver Broncos in the League's most celebrated weekly spectacle, Monday Night Football.

Since 1970, when the NFL began scheduling one game a week on Monday night, it had become a premier contest. For the most part, the NFL stages its games on Sundays, leaving a couple of dozen teams to vie for the football-watching public's attention. On Monday, though, there is only one game, and unlike Sunday's games, which are played primarily during the day, Monday's game is in prime time. Football fans the nation over, even those with no rooting interest, routinely tune in.

Mehri and Cochran harbored no hopes of their press conference gaining mention during the broadcast, but they believed if they held it in Baltimore, just forty or so miles from Mehri's office in Washington, they might attract some of the national media in town for the game.

So, for many reasons, September 30 was the ideal date to release the report. Unfortunately, that gave Mehri and Cochran only six weeks to produce it. Even before Madden ran her analysis, Mehri and Cochran hoped to compile some sort of document, if only to share stories such as Marvin Lewis'. So they already had the report's raw materials. The gulf between what they had and an acceptable end product was substantial, though, and both Mehri and Cochran were managing thriving practices, leaving neither much time to craft and polish the report. But they had little choice if they wanted to impress the media—and perhaps get the NFL's attention.

Mehri was the less busy of the two, so he took on the bulk of the work and farmed it out around his office. By late September, the report had endured countless revisions and tweaks. It was as good as it would be, not because Mehri deemed it perfect, but because time had run out. Although the document was solid, Mehri would have liked more time to tinker with it. He never lacked ideas for improving his work, and he seemed to view deadlines largely as inconvenient impediments to the creative process. If he'd had an additional month, he would have used it all, but he might have been no more satisfied with the product. To Mehri, perfection was always just around the corner. With the press conference looming, however, there were no more corners to turn. Drafting and polishing gave way to printing and copying, and by September 30 Mehri had three hundred copies stacked in his office.

The report was modestly packaged. It featured neither eye-catching graphics nor a carefully calibrated color scheme and was simply spiral-bound. It was obviously produced by lawyers and not marketing professionals, but it presented a compelling argument perfectly encapsulated by its title: *Black Coaches in the National Football League: Superior Performance, Inferior Opportunities.*

Mehri and Cochran opened the report with their motivation:

Football is "America's game." But it is more than a game. It is deeply woven into the fabric of our society and is part of our shared culture as Americans. In city after city around the country, football provides a rich common ground for a diverse fan base. Each week people of all backgrounds discuss, debate, celebrate and agonize—together—over the fortunes and disappointments of their teams. We prepared *Black Coaches in the National Football League: Superior Performance, Inferior Opportunities* because we, too, love the sport and we believe that America's Game should represent America's diversity and the best values of our society.

In the pages that followed, using statistics, qualitative comparisons, hiring cycle analyses, and respected journalists' observations, Mehri and Cochran asserted that the NFL, at least with regard to head coaches, represented neither America's diversity nor its best values. The League was, they argued, failing itself, its fans, and its nation, and it had to change.

Mehri and Cochran knew a successful, well-attended, press conference that evening might well catalyze that change, and they hoped for the best. With Cochran already in Baltimore, Mehri, his partner, Steve Skalet, and two of their paralegals packed the boxes of reports into Mehri's Subaru Outback and set off. They worked their way out of town through Washington's notorious rush-hour traffic and onto Interstate 95, which connects the nation's East Coast business centers: D.C., Baltimore, Philadelphia, New York, and Boston. Mehri had driven this highway, or taken the Amtrak train that runs roughly parallel, countless times en route to hearings, depositions, and other professional engagements, but this was different. He was new to the sports industry, and he experienced the sensations attendant to newness: excitement, anticipation, anxiety. In the end, it was excitement that trumped as they started and stopped amidst thousands of commuters escaping Washington for their bedroom communities along the highway's corridor. His reaction to Dungy's firing nine months earlier had sprouted into something big, and for much of the hour-long trip, he imagined how much bigger it could get.

Skalet, a consummate pragmatist, was focused on other, more immediate matters. He knew he would not be on the dais at the press conference. It was Mehri and Cochran's show, and he was fine with that, but he wanted to ensure that they did not overreach.

"Cyrus," he implored, "whatever happens, don't mention litigation."

Skalet was no less shrewd a lawyer than Mehri, but certainly more cautious, and since Mehri and Cochran had no plans to litigate, Skalet saw no need at that juncture to antagonize the NFL. In his view, it would poison their relationship with the League from the start and was simply unnecessary.

Though Skalet didn't know it, and Mehri didn't betray it, Skalet had stumbled upon what had become Mehri's greatest concern about the project. Mehri was no more interested than his partner in a legal showdown with the NFL, but he wondered if the NFL would respond to the report positively, or at all, without a threat. Just a few weeks earlier, Richard Lapchick, a professor at the University of Central Florida, had assured him they would not. And while Mehri deeply respected Skalet's lawyering instincts, few knew the intersection of race and sport as Lapchick did.

Although a professor, Lapchick was not an ivory tower type. He immersed himself in his work and challenged racial discrimination in sports not only through his seemingly innumerable articles and books but also through front-line activism. As a political scientist and civil rights activist during the 1960s and 1970s, Lapchick assailed South Africa's apartheid regime whenever possible, and during the late 1970s he observed that oppositionist international pressure was mounting. In 1976, the world saw pictures of South African authorities killing and maiming children in Soweto who were marching in protest of their oppression. A year later, South African officials fumbled to explain how Steve Biko, one of the nation's chief antiapartheid leaders, suffered a fatal head injury while in police custody and why, shortly after his death, the government banned virtually all dissenting expression in the country.

The South African government was on the ropes, and it sought to resurrect its image through sport. It planned to dispatch an integrated tennis team to represent South Africa against the United States in the Davis Cup, an international tennis competition to be held at Vanderbilt University in Nashville, Tennessee. Lapchick knew the image of a harmonious, multiracial South African tennis team would distract some in the international community from the regime's racially driven atrocities, and as national chairperson of the American Coordinating Committee for Equality in Sport and Society, he resolved to disrupt the match. Together with the NAACP, Lapchick's organization campaigned against the match for months, and in October 1977 Lapchick traveled to Nashville to speak on the matter. During his speech, news broke that the match's sponsors had withdrawn their financial support. Lapchick and the others who opposed South Africa's participation in the match had scored a tremendous victory, but not everyone was pleased about it.

While Lapchick was working late in his office at Virginia Wesleyan University one night several months later, two masked men confronted him and took turns beating him for almost an hour. As they terrorized him, they said only three things, but they repeated them over and over:

"Will you continue doing what you have been doing now?"

"Nigger-lover, nigger-lover."

"You know you have no business in South Africa."

During the assault, Lapchick passed out twice from the fear and the pain. When he awoke the second time, the assailants were gone, and the letters "n-i-g-e-r" (an obvious misspelling of the racial epithet "nigger") were carved into his naked stomach.

The attack terrified Lapchick, and he was never able to identify the assailants, but the incident did not shake his activist grounding. Rather, it emboldened him, and he'd vigorously battled racial discrimination, particularly in the sporting context, ever since. He had become the "conscience of sport," and when he gave advice, it paid to heed it. So when Mehri sought Lapchick's counsel and Lapchick told him that nothing short of a litigation threat would budge the NFL,

Mehri began to believe a threat might be necessary, even though he questioned whether he could carry it out. Skalet, however, was his partner and had fully supported the project from the beginning. Mehri was torn, but deep down he knew he could not refuse Skalet's request.

"No, I won't mention litigation," Mehri assured him. Nevertheless, for the rest of the trip, and even as they pulled up to Don Shula's restaurant in downtown Baltimore, Mehri feared he was making a mistake.

Shula had been a head coach in the National Football League for thirty-three years, winning two Super Bowls along the way and ultimately earning a place in the Hall of Fame. His restaurant, bedecked as it was with football memorabilia of all sorts, constituted a veritable shrine to the NFL and to coaching. It seemed an ideal location for Mehri and Cochran to unveil their report, but as the appointed hour approached it was unclear to whom they would be unveiling it. Hardly anyone was there. Mehri and Cochran expected a couple of dozen reporters and otherwise interested parties, and they hoped for more, perhaps even a roomful of people. They got six.

Notwithstanding the paltry turnout, there was no choice but to begin. So, with as much enthusiasm as possible under the circumstances, Mehri welcomed the few reporters assembled before him and quickly dove into substance. He told them about the League's historical inequities and how they persisted. He told them about Tony Dungy and Dennis Green and their unjust terminations. And he told them about Madden's statistics. All the while, he emphasized the importance that equity in sports held for the broader societal battle against racial discrimination. The NFL, he asserted, would be doing a great thing by addressing the problems the report laid bare.

After making a few additional points, Mehri gave Cochran the floor, and with the shift in speakers came a shift in tone. Cochran was less guarded in his remarks, more pointed. His comments seemed to be winding their way toward confrontation, and as they did, it became evident that neither Mehri nor Skalet had briefed

Cochran on their conversation in the car. Cochran likely would have opposed the conservative approach anyway, as his practice was built on bold legal and public relations strategies, but he might have acquiesced for unity's sake. Oblivious to their agreement, however, Cochran followed his instincts and raised the temperature. Before long, ensconced in his rhetorical groove, Cochran unleashed the show stopper. "If they don't negotiate," he resolutely exclaimed, "we will litigate."

With those seven words, Cochran essentially ended the press conference. More was said, but none of it really mattered. The reporters had their stories, and NFL officials would soon read them. There would be no slow escalation of hostilities; no faux-friendly, coffee-soaked get-to-know-you meetings. Cochran had thrown down the gauntlet, and there was no turning back.

A bit dazed, Mehri simultaneously hoped that Skalet would not be too angry and that Lapchick was right. Other than that, he figured, there was nothing to do but sweat and await the NFL's response.

He figured wrong. News of the press conference spread quickly along the journalistic grapevine, and even before Mehri made it back to his office, the phones were ringing. Jaki Lee, Mehri's temporary legal secretary, was getting increasingly frazzled with each call. It was her first day on the job, and with her boss out of the office she had anticipated the opportunity to settle in. She did not get that opportunity, and she would not get it for some time, because by happenstance, the day after the press conference Cochran launched a book tour to promote his recently released memoir, *A Lawyer's Life*. At each stop on the tour, the first question he received was about O. J. Simpson, and the second was about his challenge to the NFL. No orchestrated public relations campaign could have been more effective. Every day along the book tour trail, Cochran spoke publicly about inequities in the NFL and directed follow-up inquiries to Mehri's office. And every day in Mehri's office, Lee tried to keep up with requests for and questions about the report as well as an increasing number of pleas for just a few minutes on the phone with her boss.

Each day for the following few weeks, it seemed either Mehri or Cochran was quoted in at least one of the nation's major newspapers. They and their project were widely featured on radio and television as well, most notably on HBO's *Real Sports with Bryant Gumbel*, an hour-long sports-oriented investigative news program akin to CBS' *60 Minutes*. By the time Gumbel interviewed them, Mehri had grown as brazen as Cochran. On camera, in response to Gumbel's questioning, Mehri matter-of-factly discussed the report and concluded his remarks with sheer confidence: "There's gonna be change in the National Football League. You can mark our words on that."

Real Sports was known to chronicle only the nation's most socially significant sports stories, and by featuring the battle to diversify the NFL's head coaching ranks, Gumbel further elevated the effort's profile, which in turn further swamped Mehri's office.

Neither the Texaco case nor the Coke case had ever produced this type of buzz, and Mehri was enjoying it. So was Lee. She knew next to nothing about football, but as an African American, she felt a connection to the project and was thrilled to be involved. It was an exciting and heady time for them both and for the firm as a whole.

Then, on a day like any other, the hate began to flow. It started with a phone call from a foul-mouthed Bostonian who talked about niggers and handouts and violence before Lee hung up the phone. E-mails, letters, and calls from other disgruntled football fans followed, and as the pace of hateful communications increased, excitement yielded to concern. Some of Mehri's employees feared that the written and verbal assaults might presage something more villainous. The firm's address was publicly available, and their only protection was an unarmed guard who sat at a desk near the building's entrance checking visitors' identification. There was nothing to stop a person from entering the office with a gun and doing what he or she pleased, and with all the mail they received on a daily basis, a letter bombing was quite conceivable.

Mehri was accustomed to people not liking him and the work he did, so the threats didn't scare him. But he was responsible for his employees and for providing them a comfortable environment in which to work, and while he didn't believe the threats would amount to anything, living under threat can be disconcerting. He urged his employees to stay calm and told them what Cochran, who after the O. J. Simpson case received as much hate mail as anyone in the country, had told him: "You have to keep looking forward and not be bothered by it. Don't let it stop you."

Mehri assured his employees that the hateful communications would taper off, and eventually they did. But the public exposure that the countless interviews, the book tour, and in particular the *Real Sports* appearance provided the firm was unprecedented, and while fewer and fewer people called with threats, the phones kept ringing.

One among the many calls came from an NFL veteran, of whom Mehri had never heard, named John Wooten. Wooten, known to his friends simply as "Woots," had learned about the stand Mehri and Cochran were taking against the NFL and wanted to lend his assistance. Mehri, happy for any support they could get, welcomed it. He had no idea at the time how crucial Wooten's involvement would ultimately prove.

4

ENTER THE GODFATHER

ALTHOUGH WOOTEN WAS AN OUTSTANDING PLAYER during his ten seasons in the NFL, all but one of which he spent with the Cleveland Browns, few people outside of the League knew anything about him. He was an offensive lineman and was therefore anonymous to all but the most knowledgeable and attentive team supporters.

Other than the center, who passes the ball through his legs to the quarterback at the start of each play, an offensive lineman generally does not touch the ball unless one of his teammates fumbles and he is quick and proximate enough to recover it. The offensive lineman's job, the most thankless on the football field, is to block would-be tacklers for those who do handle the ball. While the quarterbacks and running backs for whom he blocks enjoy public adoration and vie for individual achievement awards, the offensive lineman accrues cuts and contusions while going largely unnoticed by fans. Indeed, going unnoticed usually means an offensive lineman has done his job well; it means he has not committed penalties or missed important blocks.

Wooten did not mind the anonymity that came with doing his job well. He enjoyed hard work and was uninterested in the public limelight, and he remained that way after his playing career ended.

So when Lee told Mehri a guy named John Wooten had called about the football project, Mehri could be forgiven for not knowing that the man who'd left the message was the most connected and influential African American in the NFL—the "godfather," as many called him, of the community. Mehri had no reason to know Wooten had held upper-level front office positions with the Dallas Cowboys, Philadelphia Eagles, and Baltimore Ravens, as well as at the NFL's central office at 280 Park Avenue in New York City, and that in those capacities he had developed a veritable army of friends and allies. And Mehri certainly could not have known that the semiretired Wooten wanted nothing more than to use his experience and clout to expand opportunities for African American coaches, scouts, and front office personnel in the League. Indeed, not even some of Wooten's friends fully understood the extent of his yearning to create equal opportunity—a passion that could exist only in those who once had no opportunities at all.

As a young boy in Carlsbad, New Mexico, Wooten was certain he would spend his adult years doing one of two things: collecting garbage or digging potassium sulfide in the city's potash mines. Those seemed to be his options. Nobody in Wooten's family had ever progressed beyond high school, and it seemed inconceivable that he would be the first to do so. He was a good student, but his school, Carver School, which served African Americans in grades one through twelve, was severely underresourced, and though his teachers did their best with what they had, they did not have much.

Even assuming satisfactory academic preparation, however, Wooten and his family were poor, and for them, any college would be wildly unaffordable. They had a hard enough time acquiring life's bare necessities. Wooten's mother, a single parent, labored tirelessly as a domestic worker to provide for her six children. She cleaned as many houses as she could during the week and then cleaned three churches every weekend. The work was tedious and punishing, and to help their mother, the Wooten kids transformed the church cleanings into family affairs, working alongside her until the sanctuaries were presentable for the Sunday services. Unfortunately, her earnings were insufficient to adequately support them all, so each of the Wooten children had additional jobs as well. In September and October they picked cotton in the searing New Mexico heat. When there was no cotton to pick, they shined shoes. When shoe shining dried up, they took whatever menial jobs they could to supplement the family income. Still, after pooling their money, they barely had enough to survive.

Although Wooten's future seemed preordained, he observed that opportunity existed for others. Carlsbad High School, which was not far from Wooten's home, was filled with it. Carlsbad had modern facilities—far superior to those at Carver—and a strong academic reputation. In addition, Carlsbad had a legendary athletic program. The Carlsbad Cavemen perennially challenged for state championships in basketball, football, and track and field. Carver's athletic program, on the other hand, consisted of a poorly funded basketball team and little else. Opportunity gleamed at Carlsbad High School, but Wooten could not access it. Carlsbad High and all of its opportunity were reserved for whites. The closest he could get was pretending with his friends that they were Carlsbad Cavemen as they played pickup football in the grass lot adjacent to Carlsbad's stadium while the real team competed inside. Occasionally the gate attendants allowed the youngsters in at halftime to see the remainder of the game, giving Wooten the most intimate glimpse he imagined he would ever have of the promise Carlsbad High School offered its own.

Then, for the first time in Wooten's life, after he completed the ninth grade at Carver, genuine opportunity bloomed. That autumn, when the 1952–53 academic year commenced, Carlsbad High began admitting African Americans. Wooten had done nothing to create the opportunity, and he did not know those who did. Somewhere far away, civil rights activists and lawyers had made sufficiently powerful arguments to begin unraveling segregation, and although *Brown v.*

Board of Education was yet to be decided, the Carlsbad school board and Carlsbad High School opted for integration.

Suddenly trash trucks and potash mines did not loom as ominously on the horizon. There was a chance Wooten could have something more, and he seized the opportunity with his entire being. He poured himself into his academics, absorbing everything he could, and although he had never played organized football, he tried out for the team. Almost immediately he dominated on both the offensive and defensive lines, and at the end of his sophomore season he earned all-state honors. During his junior and senior years, Wooten remained an all-state performer, all the while continuing his excellence in the classroom.

Wooten crafted himself into such a good player and such a good student that many of the nation's best football schools, such as the University of Colorado and UCLA, as well as some of its most selective academic institutions, such as Dartmouth College, fervently recruited him. In the end, Wooten chose proximity to home and enrolled at Colorado with plans to eventually attend medical school and become a physician. Wooten harbored no NFL aspirations, but after a successful academic and athletic career at Colorado, the Cleveland Browns selected him in the 1959 NFL draft's fifth round, and he entered the League as a rookie. From then until he called Mehri's office, more than forty years later, Wooten had worked in and around the NFL. Along the way, he built himself and his family a comfortable life and earned respect as a great player and then as an exceptional scout.

By any objective measure Wooten's existence bore no resemblance to what he had imagined for himself while he cleaned churches, picked cotton, and shined shoes in Carlsbad. To Wooten, however, it was only one opportunity removed. He did not enjoy contemplating what life would have been like had Carlsbad High School not integrated in 1952 and had he not received the benefits the area's teenage whites had long enjoyed. Nonetheless, when issues of racial inequity arose Wooten dutifully told his story and then flatly explained what equal opportunity meant for him: "If they don't make that integration decision, I'm dead."

But they had integrated, and Wooten was not dead. Instead, he was compulsively committed to opening opportunities for other African Americans as they were once opened for him, and in four decades with the League he had never seen the potential for change that Mehri and Cochran's report portended. He hoped the two lawyers were as serious about reforming the NFL as they appeared to be on television, and if so, he hoped Mehri would return his call.

Within days Mehri was dialing Wooten's number.

"Hello?"

Wooten's voice was deep and commanding. He sounded every bit the offensive lineman.

"Hello," Mehri responded. "This is Cyrus Mehri."

With that, the two began their first conversation, and as it turned out, they would talk nearly every day for months. With such a convergence of interests it seemed impossible not to be in close communication. Mehri was desperate to succeed with his project, and Wooten was desperate to finally catalyze the change of which he'd dreamt for decades. During their conversations, as Wooten told his story, Mehri grew to appreciate the depth of Wooten's passion for equal opportunity in the NFL and the strides he and many others had taken to further that goal.

Almost immediately after ending his playing career in 1969, Wooten explained, he entered the agent business, and worked as a players' agent for six years. The whole time, however—indeed, even during his playing days—he knew he wanted to work in an NFL team's front office. In that capacity he believed he would be able to focus on the personnel decisions that mold football franchises and, at the same time, do his best to ensure equal opportunity for African Americans hoping to work in the organization. In 1975 he got his chance. Tex Schramm, the Dallas Cowboys' president and general manager, who knew Wooten during his playing career, called and invited Wooten to assist with team operations. Wooten enthusiastically accepted, and before long he was learning the football business from Schramm. The two became good friends, but they argued mightily over issues of race in the League. Wooten, with the old

Carlsbad days forever fresh in his consciousness, steadily toiled to organize the League's off-field African American employees to push for expanded opportunities; Schramm, who believed NFL decision makers were essentially uninfluenced by race, did not view such organization as necessary.

Schramm was, it seemed, unburdened by stringent notions of formality or hierarchy, and he often walked down to Wooten's office to engage his friend in conversations, which invariably played out in the same manner. His feet propped up on Wooten's desk, leaning back in Wooten's guest chair, Schramm would query Wooten's purpose in trying to organize.

"I just don't understand what you're doing, Woots," Schramm would say, truly perplexed.

"I'm trying to make the League better," Wooten would respond. "I'm trying to make it what it should be."

"Okay. But I don't know why you have to go to all of these meetings. It's like you're saying you want to have an all-black franchise."

"I never said that. I love the NFL. I love the NFL as much as you love it, but I don't understand why we don't have any black head coaches or general managers."

Wooten would then talk about the need to expand the pool of candidates for such positions to ensure equal opportunity and, ultimately, the best selection, and Schramm would respond that it wasn't fair for anybody to tell him or any other team executive whom to hire.

"When I'm hiring, I know who I want," Schramm would insist.

"Well, of course, but we're not arguing whether you know who you want or not, we're arguing whether you got the best guy. How can you tell me you got the best guy when you haven't interviewed all these guys?"

And on and on it would go.

But whenever Wooten told Schramm he had to attend a meeting to work toward diversifying the NFL, Schramm would authorize and fund the travel. If it meant so much to Wooten, he'd concluded, he was willing to support it.

Because there were few African Americans with any real power in the NFL, the meetings were generally small and were held in whatever city and at whatever time was convenient for the greatest number of participants. Wooten was always in attendance, as were Paul "Tank" Younger and Frank Gilliam, and together they spearheaded a campaign to increase equal employment opportunity for off-field African Americans in the League.

Younger, who played football at Grambling State University and then played in the NFL from 1949 to 1958, was the oldest of the group and its unofficial dean. Although Younger starred as both a running back and a linebacker at Grambling, NFL teams at the time did not scout at historically black colleges and universities (HBCUs). Indeed, no HBCU product had ever played in the League. Needless to say, despite his ability, Younger went undrafted.

Undeterred, he managed to arrange a tryout with the Los Angeles Rams, and as he prepared for it, Grambling's longtime head coach, Eddie Robinson, flatly told him, "If you fail, there's no telling when another black athlete from a black college will get a chance to play pro football." Despite having to endure Jim Crow segregation when the Rams played games in the South early in his career, Younger did not fail, earning Pro Bowl status five times during the course of his career. After retiring, Younger joined the Rams' front office and ultimately became the first African American executive in NFL history. Among African Americans in the game, Younger was a legend.

Gilliam was not the player Wooten or Younger was, having competed in only five exhibition games with the NFL's Green Bay Packers before being cut from the team, never to play in the League again. Like Wooten and Younger, however, Gilliam had a sharp football mind, and after playing for six years in the Canadian Football League, he began coaching in Canada and then at the University of Iowa, where he had played college ball. A few years later the Minnesota Vikings hired Gilliam as a scout, and over the years he had marched up the organization's hierarchy.

As talented and accomplished as Younger, Wooten, and Gilliam were, they doubted that any of their teams would ever seriously consider promoting them to the position of general manager. Worse yet, countless equally talented African Americans seemed entirely frozen out of the League's power positions. The troika committed to do something about it, and together with the League's few other African American coaches and front office personnel, they pushed in myriad ways for change.

They did so fully aware of the hazards involved. The NFL community was small and run entirely by whites, many of whom were not as willing as Schramm to openly discuss the League's racial dynamics or accept the possibility of them shifting. Nevertheless, Younger, Wooten, Gilliam, and their comrades refused to countenance the status quo, so they accepted whatever risks their efforts posed to their long-term NFL futures. Through leveraging their relationships with friends and associates in the League, they were occasionally able to create opportunities for aspiring African American coaches on teams' coaching staffs, but their victories were isolated and their progress was slow. They wanted to make a bigger difference—to systematize change in some way—and after much discussion over the course of many meetings, they hatched an idea.

What if, they wondered, the NFL encouraged its teams' coaching staffs to work with and mentor African American college coaches during the pro teams' training camps? Such a program would have dual benefits. It would introduce NFL teams to coaching talent with which they were likely unfamiliar and it would familiarize the college coaches, many of whom harbored NFL ambitions, with the professional game, thereby improving those coaches' chances of competing for NFL jobs. Inspired by the idea's promise, Younger, Wooten, and Gilliam, together with the Washington Redskins' assistant general manager, Bobby Mitchell, and a few others, traveled to New York and proposed the idea to NFL Commissioner Pete Rozelle.

Rozelle had been observing the group's efforts and had grown increasingly attentive to their cause and sympathetic to the resistance they faced, but there was no indication when they convened at the NFL's headquarters that he was prepared to support such an ambitious project. And absent Younger's involvement, he might well not have. Before becoming commissioner, however, Rozelle had worked in the Rams' front office, first as a publicist and then eventually as the general manager, and while there he and Younger had forged a friendship. For much of the meeting in New York, while Wooten, Gilliam, Mitchell, and the others talked among themselves at one of the NFL's large conference room tables, Younger and Rozelle, both smokers, huddled out of earshot across the room puffing on their cigarettes and discussing the proposal. In the end, trusting Younger's judgment, Rozelle decided to implement the group's idea, initiating what became the Black Coaches Visitation Program.

Under the program, the League paid for numerous HBCUs' entire coaching staffs to spend portions of the summer at NFL off-season camps. They sat in on coaching meetings, assisted with drills, and discussed the merits of various on-field strategies. Few African American coaches had ever had such access to the NFL's inner workings.

Not everyone in the NFL community cared for the program, but many applauded it and expressed their support both to Rozelle and to the African American front office pioneers who originated it. Among the impressed was San Francisco 49ers head coach Bill Walsh. Walsh was close friends with Dr. Harry Edwards, the University of California academic who had dedicated his career to forwarding equal opportunity through sports and who had inspired Tommie Smith and John Carlos' 1968 Olympic medal stand protest. Through conversations with Edwards, Walsh had grown increasingly disconcerted with the dearth of African American coaches in the NFL, and when he learned of Wooten's efforts, he committed to assisting in any way he could. As such, in 1987 he created his own personal minority internship program, soliciting from Wooten the names of promising young African American coaches and then hiring them as quality control assistants with the goal of preparing them for higher-level positions on his staff or elsewhere in the League.

The Black Coaches Visitation Program and Walsh's internship program, which the League ultimately adopted and expanded, served to markedly increase the number of minority coaches in the NFL.

Once in the League, though, the coaches for the most part stagnated as position coaches or occasionally as coordinators, with just a few attaining head coaching positions. Persuading NFL franchise owners to accept interns and low-level African American coaches was one thing, but convincing them to consider hiring African American coaches to lead their teams was quite another.

Wooten, Younger, and Gilliam continued to convene meetings, sometimes attracting fifty or more people, but they were, as Wooten told Mehri, largely "screaming and hollering" sessions. The group took no concerted action, as many attendees feared reprisals, and aside from anecdotes, they had no objective evidence to prove they were suffering systemic discrimination. In short, they felt they had no leverage. As Wooten explained over the course of his many conversations with Mehri, however, Mehri and Cochran's report appeared to provide just the leverage he and his allies had long sought. Humble as always, Wooten expressed his pleasure to be joining Mehri and Cochran's movement. By then, however, Mehri had learned enough about Wooten to know it was the other way around. Mehri and Cochran were joining Wooten's movement, and they were happy to do so.

As connected as Wooten was in the NFL community, however, and despite the numerous friendships he enjoyed with high-level executives in the League's central office, he had no idea how the League would respond to the report. Nobody did, not even the League executives, who, as Mehri and Wooten were getting acquainted, were working through the report and trying to plot their course of action.

5

THE ROONEY RULE

MANY ASPIRING SPORTS LAWYERS, uninterested in seemingly more mundane legal pursuits, spend their collegiate and law school years fanatically priming themselves to one day represent players, teams, or leagues. Others are frustrated athletes—just a few inches too short or a few steps too slow to live their dreams—who, through the law, get as close to those dreams as possible. But for some sports lawyers there is no intent, no pursuit. They simply stumble into what scores of their former classmates and colleagues desperately crave.

Jeff Pash fit that third category.

Nothing in his life experience suggested he would one day be general counsel to the nation's most popular and powerful sports enterprise. He was not particularly athletic. He had never played organized football and had played only a bit of Little League baseball as a child. And at Harvard Law School, he had no sports lawyering ambitions. In fact, aside from a general interest in litigation, he had no idea what he wanted to do with his legal career after graduating. So upon receiving his law degree in 1980, he headed off to Covington

& Burling, a prestigious, white-shoe, Washington, D.C.-based law firm with a diverse practice, open to whatever work awaited him.

For recent law school graduates, joining a firm without expressing a practice preference is a risky proposition. Those without preferences are generally assigned to work for whichever of the firm's partners need staffing assistance at the time, and those most likely to need assistance are often short-staffed for a reason. Some are unyielding taskmasters from whom associates flee the moment they can extricate themselves. Others are pleasant enough but repel associates with their frightfully boring practices. Indeed, many new associates, particularly former summer interns familiar with the firm's partners and their client rosters, express practice preferences just to avoid, to the extent possible, ogres and mind-numbing work.

Of course, sometimes a humane partner with a compelling practice has an opening, and a new associate, otherwise at the mercy of the firm's assigning mechanism, is tapped to fill it. To Jeff Pash's great fortune, when he arrived at Covington, one of the firm's most respected partners, Paul Tagliabue, needed additional associate assistance in representing the NFL as outside counsel.

Tagliabue was demanding but reasonable, and for nine years Pash apprenticed under him. In 1989, however, Pete Rozelle stepped down as NFL commissioner, and the League's owners selected Tagliabue to fill Rozelle's shoes, leaving Pash and a few other Covington attorneys to handle the NFL's legal needs. Shortly thereafter, when the National Hockey League sought a general counsel, Tagliabue encouraged Pash to pursue the opportunity, and a few years after that, in 1996, when the NFL needed the same, Tagliabue brought him aboard.

Six years into his tenure with the League, Pash still loved his job, but not for the reasons so many lawyers salivated at the thought of being the NFL's general counsel. Neither the celebrity of the position nor the intimate access it offered to professional football meant much to Pash. Indeed, when he attended games he sat in the stands among the other spectators rather than in any of the luxury boxes to which he easily could have secured admittance. And after games, even the

Super Bowl, which is just as much a party as it is a football contest, he never joined friends, colleagues, and the victorious team down on the field. "They didn't need me there," Pash would say, explaining why he routinely declined what to many would be priceless opportunities. Pash's job was not to meet and greet but to protect the NFL's diverse and complex interests, and that is what he enjoyed. He was a lawyer's lawyer, and he took pride in his craft.

When Pash received Mehri and Cochran's report on the heels of Cochran's litigation threat, therefore, he scrutinized it from all angles. He examined the statistics the lawyers highlighted, their qualitative claims, and Madden's analysis, which was attached as Appendix B. Like a bomb squad technician, Pash patiently and painstakingly assessed the threat the report posed until finally concluding that the NFL had little to fear in the courtroom. Because the NFL had never directed clubs' hiring decisions, Pash did not see how any court could find the League liable for the racial disproportionalities the report highlighted. Indeed, in his view, the issue was so obvious that he was certain Mehri and Cochran saw it as well, leading him to deduce the report was a classic litigation bluff, prepared more for the media than for the legal process.

Had Mehri and Cochran been there to advocate, hyperbolically or otherwise, the strength of their potential case, perhaps they could have shaken Pash's confidence that any litigation attempt would be futile, and if so, perhaps Pash would have continued viewing the report as a potential litigation building block.

However, with nothing to convince him otherwise, Pash remained confident that the report was, as a legal matter, relatively harmless, so he lowered his lawyerly hackles and gave it another, less defensive read. In doing so, he found much to admire. Mehri and Cochran were not crafting a controversy from whole cloth. They were highlighting an issue of which he was well aware and about which he was concerned. Moreover, they were not simply throwing stones. In addition to their criticisms, Pash was pleased to see, they presented recommended action items. Although Pash did not believe the report fairly represented the League's equal opportunity efforts and although he worried about the inevitable media fallout, he chose to view the report primarily as constructive criticism, albeit unsolicited—potentially capable of helping the NFL to diversify its teams' coaching staffs.

As concerned as Pash had grown about equal opportunity for the League's coaches of color, the NFL's chief operating officer, Roger Goodell, was even more concerned, if only because he had been struggling with the issue for far longer. Just a year after graduating from college in 1981, Goodell joined the NFL as an intern. The following year he took a full-time public relations position with the League's New York Jets, and in 1984 he rejoined the NFL's staff, this time as a public relations assistant. Goodell never again left the League. He was, essentially, a lifer, slowly climbing up the chain of command until in 2001 Tagliabue appointed him COO.

Among Goodell's original duties during his first few years with the League was to help teams diversify their workforces. The NFL had neither a diversity policy nor a formalized process through which it sought to diversify, but there was a sense at 280 Park Avenue that, aside from teams' players, people of color were sorely underrepresented in the League. Goodell's superiors charged him with identifying talented candidates of color who would thrive in leadership positions with NFL teams, including coaching positions, if granted opportunities.

Goodell relished the task. Since childhood, his father, who served in the United States House of Representatives for ten years and in the United States Senate for two, had schooled his son on the importance of equal opportunity. He explained that in addition to inevitably producing the best outcomes, giving everyone a fair chance regardless of race was simply the right thing to do and that maintaining one's principles on such important issues was crucial. As impactful as the elder Goodell's words were on his boy, his actions proved even more so. As a moderate-to-conservative Republican congressman and then senator from New York, Charles Goodell initially had a bright political future. Over time, though, he grew disturbed about America's increasing military involvement in Vietnam and began publicly challenging the Republican establishment, including President Richard Nixon, on the issue. Vice President Spiro T. Agnew and other Republican heavyweights counterattacked, painting Goodell as a disloyal "radical liberal" and, by demonizing him among his conservative constituents, essentially drove him out of office. The elder Goodell never regretted his stand, and his son, who counted among his prize possessions the original letter his father sent Nixon opposing the war, never forgot his father's lesson in conviction.

Armed with his father's early guidance, the younger Goodell had tried throughout his career with the NFL to open employment opportunities for those who might otherwise be overlooked, and although he had achieved some success, he knew there remained much to be done.

Tagliabue, like Goodell and Pash, recognized the League's poor diversity record on the head coaching front, and while he knew that racial prejudice, whether subconscious or not, had certainly contributed to that record over the years, the commissioner, like his COO and his general counsel, ascribed the League's recent woes less to overt racism than to timing.

The NFL's head coaching carousel had long been a mad scramble. Each year around the end of the season, several teams fired their head coaches and immediately entered the market for replacements. Upon firing its head coach, however, a team did not always know which other teams would enter the head coaching market, when they would do so, or which candidates they would most desire. Celerity, therefore, proved a powerful hiring weapon. Signing a head coach quickly often meant doing so before other job opportunities, some of which that head coach might ultimately have preferred, materialized. Even assuming no competition for candidates, one NFL season's end marks the next season's beginning, and clubs tended to hire their new coaches as soon as possible so as to commence preparations for the following year. Teams pursuing deliberative, comprehensive head coaching searches appeared to lose out in the scramble, rendering such hiring approaches increasingly obsolete.

Instead, loath to waste time, an owner or general manager with a head coaching vacancy often targeted a coach or two he knew and in whom he had confidence, hastily conducted interviews, and rushed an offer onto the table. Through the end of the previous season, every owner and general manager in the League had been white, and because the coaches with whom they were most familiar and in whom they had the greatest confidence were generally white, teams' brain trusts rarely considered candidates of color.

Tagliabue believed that this timing dynamic and the myopia it incentivized were largely responsible for the difficulty candidates of color faced in pursuing head coaching opportunities, and he had been trying for years to slow the coaching carousel's pace. Most recently, he had invited a consulting firm, Russell Reynolds Associates, to meet with the League's owners to urge them to search for head coaches as they might search for executives in their other business interests. If they did not make snap judgments and partially informed decisions when hiring chief executive officers, the consultants insisted, they should not do so when hiring head coaches. It was simply bad business.

But the unique nature of head coach hiring seemed to trump such considerations, and the coaching carousel proceeded just as quickly the season after the Reynolds presentation as it had the season before. Mehri and Cochran's report starkly highlighted Tagliabue's concerns about equal opportunity and further convinced him that a slower carousel was necessary to achieve that end.

Assured by Pash that the League did not face a substantial litigation threat, conscious of the negative publicity Mehri and Cochran's continued media blitz could cause, and with essentially nothing to lose, Tagliabue decided to open a dialogue and authorized his legal staff to invite Mehri and Cochran to the League's offices.

Mehri was thrilled, but none of the dates the NFL offered over the following several weeks were available on Cochran's calendar, creating for Mehri a dilemma: postpone the meeting and lose momentum or proceed without Cochran. From the beginning, Mehri recognized that the price of involving Cochran in his project would be Cochran's occasional absence. Cochran was insanely busy—at all times seemingly pulled in hundreds of directions—and Mehri knew he would sometimes have to push forward alone. This, it appeared, would be one of those times. Cochran urged Mehri to accept the appointment, and Mehri did.

Mehri did not relish the idea of meeting the NFL's lawyers alone, although he was not afraid to do so. Rather, he felt that alone he would be suboptimally equipped, as he worked best when vetting ideas with others. At his office, if his partner, Steve Skalet, was not around, Mehri bounced ideas and brainstorms off his associates. If he could not find one of his associates, he would turn to his paralegals. A sounding board was crucial to Mehri's creative process, and he did not want to be without one when he visited the NFL's headquarters. In Cochran's absence, Mehri asked Lapchick, who would provide as good a sounding board as anyone, to join him, and Lapchick agreed.

Like Mehri, Pash was strategic about composing the group that would sit on his side of the table at the meeting. He did not think it appropriate for Tagliabue to be involved; he preferred more of a buffer between Mehri and his boss. Yet he understood the importance of convincing Mehri that the NFL was sincere in its desire to open a line of communication, and he wanted the meeting to project that sincerity. As such, he knew Tom Williamson had to be in the room.

Williamson, a partner at Covington with whom both Tagliabue and Pash had worked closely while there, had been since their respective departures meeting some of the NFL's outside counsel needs. Williamson's familiarity with the NFL and his relationship with Tagliabue and Pash only partially drove their interest in seeking his help, however. His relationship with Mehri was the clincher.

Williamson was one of the nation's most well-connected litigators and counted among his friends Bill Clinton, with whom he had hitchhiked around Europe when the two were Rhodes scholars together at Oxford University. Aside from two stints in government, one of which was spent as President Clinton's solicitor of labor, Williamson had been at Covington since 1974, and it seemed he knew, and had earned the respect of, every lawyer in Washington, D.C., Mehri included. In fact, Mehri so respected Williamson that although Williamson made his living representing large corporations against employees' lawsuits, Mehri had, in the wake of his successful settlement with Texaco, been pleased that the court appointed Williamson to chair the Texaco Task Force on Equality and Fairness, which ensured Texaco's adherence to the settlement terms.

Mehri knew neither Pash nor Harold Henderson—the NFL's executive vice president for labor relations and chairman of the NFL Management Council Executive Committee, who would also attend the meeting—and had no reason to trust either of them. Pash viewed Williamson's presence, therefore, as crucial to establishing a productive working relationship.

On October 22, 2002, the appointed date for the meeting, Mehri and Lapchick stepped out of the elevator on the seventeenth floor of 280 Park Avenue and were immediately assaulted by all things football. Behind the reception desk, which was emblazoned with the NFL's shield-shaped red, white, and blue logo, hung rows of gleaming football helmets representing various League teams, and every corner of the room seemed to house a remarkable item of NFL memorabilia. Tom Landry's feather-adorned fedora, which he wore during his two-plus decades pacing the Dallas Cowboys' sidelines, was secured in glass against one wall. A Green Bay Packers jacket once belonging to legendary Packers head coach Vince Lombardi was displayed against another. Hall of Fame players' jerseys were in the reception area as well, as were conference championship trophies. It was a football lover's paradise, and Mehri was a football lover. Lapchick's father had played and coached professional basketball, and Lapchick himself had spent decades studying professional and collegiate sports, but it was all new to Mehri, and he could have been forgiven for gawking. But starry-eyed sightseers do not make good impressions on potential adversaries, so Mehri ignored the surroundings and focused on his task.

The conference room in which the five men met was, relative to the reception area, nondescript, and there were no finger foods or soft drinks. It was bare-bones, suggesting the NFL was dispensing with pleasantries and intent on getting straight to business. The meeting was nevertheless far more cordial than it could have been, in part because Pash had calculated correctly. While Williamson's presence did not exactly comfort Mehri—after all, Williamson was still a defense lawyer—it at least convinced him a sincere conversation, rather than a snow job, was in the offing.

Everyone in the room participated, but Mehri and Pash emerged as the principal discussants. Pash clearly wanted to convey, both as a matter of fact and as a matter of organizational pride, that the NFL had worked for years to ensure equal opportunity for African American coaches. He detailed the League's efforts, beginning with the work in which Goodell had been involved in the early 1980s and continuing through to the still-existent Bill Walsh–inspired NFL Minority Fellowship Program. He also spoke about multiple meetings he, Commissioner Tagliabue, and other NFL executives had attended over the years to discuss the issue with African American coaches in the League. In addition, he described League initiatives—such as the Reynolds presentation and coaching symposia designed to facilitate interaction between previously unacquainted coaches and owners—that were not specifically geared toward Mehri's concerns but which the League hoped would open owners' minds to theretofore unconsidered head coaching candidates. The NFL, Pash assured Mehri, was aware of the disproportionalities Mehri had documented and was committed to addressing them.

Mehri, through personal study and Wooten's tutelage, had become an expert on the NFL's efforts, so nothing Pash said surprised him. Still, Pash's earnestness was obvious and encouraging. So Mehri tried not to sound dismissive when he acknowledged the League's hard work but argued that it was ultimately insufficient.

To truly create equal coaching opportunity in the NFL, Mehri insisted, the League had to do more. It had to, in Mehri's view, unequivocally impress upon its member clubs that equal coaching opportunity was a top priority, and Mehri knew just how it could do so. Mehri called it the Fair Competition Resolution. The resolution was multifaceted, but it revolved around the concept of racially diverse candidate slates. In essence, he explained, the NFL should require that its teams interview at least one person of color (Mehri was careful to not limit the proposal to African Americans, as Latino and Asian coaching aspirants, although far fewer in number, seemed at an opportunity deficit as well) when considering head coaching candidates.

Under the resolution, teams would be able to interview an unlimited number of candidates and would not have to offer the candidate of color any special accommodation, just an interview of the quality other candidates enjoyed. Mehri had seen such mandated diverse candidate slates working to great effect in diversifying upper-level corporate management in various industries. He recognized, of course, that in the case of an unapologetically bigoted decision maker, diverse candidate slates were ineffective and equal opportunity often required the decision maker's ouster. Generally, however, Mehri observed that when a corporate executive sat down to discuss an area of common interest with a candidate of a different race who might have otherwise been overlooked for an interview—whether the topic be how to best brand a soft drink or how to improve the quality of tires—preconceptions and biases tended to weaken and the interview became more meaningful than the executive initially might have imagined it would be.

Mehri believed the same would happen in the NFL, and that good-faith interviews were all the League's assistant coaches and co-ordinators of color needed to start landing head coaching jobs. Once in the door, with the opportunity to talk football, he asserted, they would dazzle club decision makers. Mehri was quick to point out, though, that under his proposal no team would be forced to hire from a racially diverse candidate slate. A team could opt out simply by forfeiting a first-round draft pick.

Until then, the NFL contingent had been for the most part listening intently, apparently intrigued by Mehri's idea. They knew that Major League Baseball had a few years earlier encouraged its teams to conduct more inclusive searches when seeking to hire managers, and although Mehri was lobbying for a formal mandate rather than mere encouragement, the idea was not entirely unrealistic. The two words "draft pick," however, changed everything. Henderson, in particular, could not contain his incredulity. Of the three NFL representatives in the room, Henderson had been most skeptical of Mehri and Cochran's report. He recognized the validity of their basic equal opportunity thesis, but he initially viewed them as "headline-grabbing, self-serving outsiders," more interested in using the issue to bolster their legal practices than in actually helping the NFL improve. Mehri's presentation thus had come as a pleasant surprise, as Mehri was obviously sincere and seemed both friendly and knowledgeable about the NFL. But draft pick forfeiture was in Henderson's view wildly inappropriate, so much so that when Mehri proposed it, Henderson seemed momentarily to convulse, as if a powerful surge of electricity coursed through his body, and then he erupted. Draft picks, Henderson explained, trying to restrain himself, were like gold in the NFL. On rare occasions the League had seized teams' picks, but only to penalize an ill-gotten competitive advantage, such as exceeding the cap the League placed on teams' player salaries. Under such circumstances the draft pick seizure constituted a competitive disadvantage that served to counterbalance the wrongly acquired competitive advantage.

Henderson considered Mehri's proposal patently absurd and believed there was no chance the team owners would even consider it. In fact, for Henderson the proposal alone was enough to damage the credibility of the entire equal opportunity effort. It was obvious Henderson would fight to the death on the issue, and although Pash and Williamson said little, they were clearly in Henderson's camp.

Moving Mehri off one of his ideas was not easy, but Henderson had done it. Draft pick forfeiture was an obvious nonstarter, and Mehri did not mention it again for the meeting's duration. The underlying idea of racially diverse candidate slates, however, seemed to gain some traction, even with Henderson, and by the time Mehri and Lapchick walked back out past the various football accoutrements, rode the elevator down to the lobby, and reentered the New York bustle, Mehri felt relieved. Until that day he had not known what to expect from the NFL. On more occasions than he cared to count, he'd sat in conference rooms with executives who were intransigent on issues of diversity, and in some cases quite clearly racist. The people he'd just left were neither. They wanted to improve. They simply seemed not to know how. As Mehri waited for a taxicab on Park Avenue, he replayed portions of the meeting in his mind and grew increasingly certain that he'd made progress.

He was right. Although the NFL brass was not prepared to take immediate action on the matter, they found the report as well as Mehri's presentation sufficiently compelling that they sent copies to each League team and committed to dedicating a portion of the October owners' meeting, which would convene a week later over two days in New York City, to discussing the report and its ramifications. When the owners gathered, each had presumably read the report and given it some thought, but one among them, Pittsburgh Steelers owner Dan Rooney, arrived ready to act.

Rooney was an icon even among his fellow owners. Dan's father, Art, had founded the Steelers, one of the NFL's most successful and beloved franchises, in 1933, and in 1960 appointed Dan director of personnel. Since then the younger Rooney had been deeply involved with the Steelers organization, and as time passed he became increasingly involved in League governance, developing into perhaps the most respected man in professional football. Although relatively short and slight and, by 2002, into his eighth decade of life, Rooney was a giant.

At the meeting, Rooney presented Tagliabue with a letter that made two basic points: (1) the issues the report presented were important and required attention, and (2) because it was the League's teams that make hiring decisions, the teams, not the League office, should take responsibility for addressing the report's concerns. Following from those two points, Rooney proposed that Tagliabue create a committee of team owners to explore diversity in the League, and before the meeting adjourned, Tagliabue did just that. The committee's members were among the League's most progressive and freethinking owners: Arthur Blank of the Atlanta Falcons, Pat Bowlen of the Denver Broncos, Stan Kroenke of the St. Louis Rams, Jeff Lurie of the Philadelphia Eagles, and of course Dan Rooney, who served as chair. In addition, to assist the owners' committee, Tagliabue appointed a committee of club executives to explore the same issues: Ray Anderson of the Atlanta Falcons, Terry Bradway of the New York Jets, Rich McKay of the Tampa Bay Buccaneers, Bill Polian of the Indianapolis Colts, and Ozzie Newsome, whom the Baltimore Ravens had just made the first African American general manager in League history. The executives, like the owners, were generally progressive thinkers.

The constitution of the committees was no accident. Tagliabue knew that for the committees to be effective, it was important that their members share at least a basic commitment to the diversity ideal, and each of the appointed individuals did. They were certainly not all of one mind, but they were all inclined to take the report, and the League's response to the report, seriously.

Of the committees' members, Anderson offered a unique perspective and was particularly anxious to get started. Before joining the Falcons organization, he had served as an agent for many of the League's aspiring African American head coaching candidates as well as the League's only two African American head coaches, Tony Dungy and Herman Edwards. As such, he knew well the race-infused obstacles they had to overcome in securing promotions, and he was unafraid to publicly discuss the double standards they faced. Featured in the *Real Sports* episode Bryant Gumbel dedicated to exploring Mehri and Cochran's campaign, Anderson matter-of-factly explained: "As African Americans in this country, we've always had to face that challenge, Bryant. You've got to be better to get to the very top. Unfortunately, that's part of our society and some of that exists in the NFL. There's no doubt." Anderson did not profess to know the solution, but he was intimately familiar with the problem, and he was prepared to share his insights with both the executives' and owners' committees.

As Rooney, Anderson, and the committees' other members organized to address the equal opportunity issues the League had long battled and with which they were now confronted, Tagliabue dispatched Williamson to open a dialogue with Mehri. Williamson was pleased with the assignment, as he believed Tagliabue was not posturing, but rather sought an earnest, solution-oriented conversation. Williamson felt so because Tagliabue had on numerous occasions over the course of their time together at Covington evidenced his commitment to racial justice, most pointedly during the South African Airways episode of 1985.

Williamson had not planned to be a lifelong Covington & Burling lawyer. Like most new law firm associates, he initially viewed it as an experience-building opportunity that might ultimately launch him toward something else. As the years passed, though, he grew to like the firm and his place in it. Still, one aspect of the firm's practice deeply vexed him. Covington represented South African Airways, the nation's government-owned airline, and the firm was therefore, in Williamson's view, aiding South Africa's apartheid state. The thought sickened Williamson, an African American, and he promised himself that if he ever became a partner at the firm, he would do something about it.

Sure enough, Williamson made partner, and within weeks he had gathered a group of like-minded partners and mounted a campaign to end the South African Airways client relationship. Disinviting a client on ideological grounds was virtually unheard of at Covington, and convincing the partnership to do so promised to be challenging, but Williamson was committed to his goal, and with Tagliabue among his strongest allies, he achieved it.

Over the years, Williamson had often recalled Tagliabue's passion in advocating that the firm withdraw from representing South African Airways and firmly believed Tagliabue's efforts were crucial to the campaign's success. When Tagliabue told Williamson he wanted to increase equal opportunity in the NFL, therefore, Williamson was pleased to help.

Mehri, for his part, was glad to receive Williamson's call proposing further discussions both because he trusted that Williamson would engage the issue in good faith and because Williamson was a consummate diplomat. He was mild-mannered and measured in his speech, choosing his words with such precision that it was exceedingly difficult to misconstrue his statements. He was an asset to any potentially conflagrant conversation. Cochran, deferring to Mehri's judgment, was comfortable with Williamson as well.

In the days since Mehri and Cochran sent the NFL their report, however, their fledging movement had grown, with Wooten recruiting several of his closest allies to assist the effort. Wooten's troops constituted a who's who of NFL greats, including former Green Bay Packers defensive lineman Willie Davis, former Kansas City Chiefs linebacker Willie Lanier, and former San Diego Chargers tight end Kellen Winslow, all of whom were in the Pro Football Hall of Fame.

As eager as each was to press the NFL for reform, Winslow was exceptionally so and was thoroughly uninterested in working through Williamson or any other intermediary. Those who knew Winslow best were not surprised. Even friends described him as headstrong, and he rarely shied away from confrontation. When there was a battle to fight he engaged it directly, on the front lines, refusing to lose. His personality struck some as abrasive and others as endearing in its sincerity, but whatever one's view, it undoubtedly served him well on the field. Winslow showed as much spirit—as much "heart," as they say in sports—as anybody in professional football, and if anyone doubted it, the Chargers-Dolphins playoff game in Miami on January 2, 1982, was exhibit A.

In that game, which the Chargers won in overtime, Winslow delivered one of the greatest individual performances in NFL history. Despite being treated throughout the game for severe cramps, dehydration, a pinched nerve in his shoulder, and a gash in his lower lip requiring stitches, Winslow caught thirteen passes for 166 yards, scored a touchdown, and blocked a last-second Dolphin field goal attempt that would have given Miami the victory.

Even after Winslow retired, that spirit continued to drive him. He noticed almost immediately what he believed to be a disparity in the off-field football opportunities former players of different races received. Whites he knew had made the transition to post-playing careers with relative ease, but in his assessment it was substantially more difficult for him and other African Americans. To Winslow, racial discrimination was the clear culprit, and after nearly a decade of seemingly race-blind adulation from legions of fans, he found its harsh reality crushing. As he later explained:

> As long as I was on the field of play I was treated and viewed differently than most African-American men in this country. Because of my physical abilities, society accepted and even catered to me. Race was not an issue. Then reality came calling. After a nine-year career in the National Football League, I stepped into the real world and realized . . . I was just another nigger . . . the images and stereotypes that applied to African-American men in this country attached to me.

Winslow's revelation led him to channel his talents toward exposing inequity in sports, and he became relentless in that pursuit. People unfamiliar with Winslow's mission got an earful on July 29, 1995, when he delivered his Hall of Fame induction speech. The Hall allots each inductee seven minutes for remarks. Winslow took more than twenty. He knew his induction provided a singular opportunity to share his views with the thousands assembled in Canton, Ohio, for the ceremony as well as the many more watching on television, and he utilized it to highlight the discrimination the League's players of color faced when seeking to transition from the football field into the sport's power positions. Some observers, even some who supported Winslow's arguments, found the speech inappropriate for the occasion. Others applauded his principled stand and the courage it required. But nobody who watched the induction ceremonies was left wondering where Winslow stood on the issue of equal opportunity in the NFL. He wanted justice, he wanted it immediately, and he had little patience for protocol or delay.

Voicing concerns with the NFL through Williamson was in Winslow's view a colossal waste of time, and when Mehri organized a conference call between Williamson and Wooten's group, Winslow made that opinion abundantly clear. Williamson opened the call with a brief introduction, explaining that his role was to listen to the participants' concerns but that he had no authority at that point to make any decisions.

Winslow jumped in immediately: "Why are we talking with you, then?"

The question startled Williamson, who, offended and uninterested in justifying his role, said little in response. Williamson's refusal to answer only further annoyed Winslow, concretizing his view that speaking with Williamson was useless. Some of the other NFL veterans tried to calm Winslow, and the call continued, but to little effect. Williamson began to speak of the NFL's commitment to equal opportunity and rehashed some of what Pash had said back in New York about the programs the League had implemented over the years, but Winslow again grew impatient.

"The programs you're talking about have been tried and are a waste of time," he interrupted. "It's an insult to our intelligence that you would talk about that stuff."

That effectively ended the call. Had Winslow and Williamson met under different circumstances, the two men might have been friends or at least cordial acquaintances. On that call, though, Winslow, smarting from years of frustration with the NFL, and Williamson, hired to represent the League but without final authority to act, could not amicably coexist. More calls would follow, however, and while the two men never developed a close relationship, their dedication to the same goal—expanded opportunity for coaches of color in the NFL—allowed them to work together productively.

Williamson emerged from the calls convinced that the best means of bringing about that goal was the mandated use of diverse candidate slates for head coaching interviews, the cornerstone of Mehri's Fair Competition Resolution proposal. The challenge, as Williamson put it, was "to get the NFL to take ownership of the diverse candidate slate solution even though it, from an adversarial point of view, was tainted by having come from the folks who published a report to pillory the League." Williamson embraced the challenge, and when Tagliabue invited him to meet with the owners' committee and the executives' committee to share his view on how the League should proceed, Williamson prepared what he likened to a closing argument.

Even before meeting with the owners and executives, Williamson doubted he would achieve success in pressing the case for diverse candidate slates, because he sensed that the committee members, as well as the League officials, were initially disinclined toward the idea. The primary concern, as Williamson understood it, was that the mandated interviews would in most cases devolve into transparent, pro forma shams, wasting the clubs' time and potentially stigmatizing the candidates of color.

Williamson was not afraid to present an unpopular view, so despite what he imagined would be a hard sell, he launched his argument. He began by espousing the benefits of diverse candidate slates, touching on many of the points Mehri had made to him over the past several weeks, but before long the conversation turned to his audience's misgivings—the very misgivings Williamson had anticipated—and Williamson assumed a defensive posture.

"You all are concerned about sham interviews, I understand that," he stated in an attempt to counter the tide, "but first of all, let's be real. Most interviews for important positions are sham interviews in the sense you're talking about, because somebody most often has already made up their mind who they really want for the important position. There's nothing new about that." It was rare that every interviewee for a job stood an equal chance of prevailing, he contended, so his proposal was really not so radical. Moreover, he asserted, "there are times when people think they are conducting a sham interview and it turns out they are so impressed with the person they thought was the sham interview candidate that they change their minds." In other words, he continued, an apparent sham interview is only a sham when the interviewer treats it as such. When the interviewer takes the interview seriously, Williamson assured the owners and executives in the room, the interviewer is often pleasantly surprised, and sometimes the sham interviewee emerges as the strongest candidate.

At some point during his defense of the diverse candidate slate, Williamson turned to an anecdote he hoped would prove useful. Williamson explained that years earlier, former secretary of the army Clifford Alexander reviewed a list of general officer candidates and noticed that it contained no minorities' names. Frustrated, he announced he would not move forward until he received a more inclusive list. Upon receiving and scrutinizing the new list, Alexander settled on one of the newly added candidates. The selection? Colin Powell, an African American, who by all accounts developed into an unmitigated professional success in the United States Army and one of the most respected individuals in American public life. Williamson contended that while Powell won the position, the army—by selecting a superior candidate who, but for the diverse candidate slate process, would have gone unnoticed—was the true winner. Utilizing a diverse candidate slate in searching for a head coach gave each team the chance to strengthen its organization and therefore improve its chances of winning football games. Rejecting the opportunity to do so, Williamson suggested, would be unwise.

Finally, well aware that his other arguments might not have persuaded anybody in the room, Williamson retreated to the bottom line. He recognized that Tagliabue had stocked the two committees with individuals who shared Tagliabue's dedication to equal opportunity, so he confronted them with a question to which he knew the answer. "If you're so concerned and upset about how flawed this proposed approach is," he concluded, "what better idea do you have?" In twenty years of trying, the people in that room and others around the NFL had failed to ensure equal opportunity for the League's head coaching candidates. There were no better ideas, and Williamson knew it. His proposal was all they had.

Still, after the meeting, as Williamson rode the Amtrak train back from New York to Washington, he was certain he had not succeeded in his mission. When he concluded his presentation, nobody had clapped. There were no pats on the back and no whispered assurances that he had made good sense, and so he had no reason for optimism. But his next conversation with Pash yielded a surprise. Some of the owners and executives were talking with increasing enthusiasm about diverse candidate slates, and they wanted additional input from Williamson.

Throughout the fall of 2002, the committees continued to meet on the issue, sometimes with Williamson present, sometimes not, and as they did, scores of commentators, professional and amateur alike, engaged in a parallel debate through the press.

Nobody outside of the NFL community knew the details of the owners' and executives' talks, but Mehri and Cochran's report, which by then had been widely disseminated, sparked strong reactions. Some commentators, aware of the League's historic diversity challenges and convinced by Mehri and Cochran's statistics, supported their campaign. Scores of others attacked the report as advocating unfair affirmative action, and some argued that if African American coaches deserved a preference, so too did white players. Luke Smith of the *Michigan Daily* presented perhaps the most creative example of such an argument. Lampooning Mehri and Cochran's report, Smith wrote "an open letter to Paul Tagliabue," claiming to attach a study titled *White Wide-outs and the National Football League: Historical Brilliance, Recent Failure—the White Man's Quest for Respect at the Wide Receiver Position.* "When given an opportunity, white athletes at the wide receiver position have done their jobs dutifully," Smith wrote. "My study shows conclusively that white wide receivers are being held to higher standards."

Of course there was no such study, and Smith seemed to be writing at least to some extent in jest, but his central point mirrored a constant refrain among those attacking Mehri and Cochran's report: what about the underrepresented white players? If the NFL were to grant African American coaches preferences, the argument went, it should do the same for white players, who occupied less than 35 percent of the League's roster spots.

The argument severely frustrated Mehri and Cochran because it mischaracterized their report. They did not view their report as advocating for affirmative action, at least not in the traditional sense. Their proposal for diverse candidate slates neither preferred coaches of color nor disadvantaged white coaches in vying for head coaching positions. The proposal did not bear on hiring at all. It merely required that before hiring, all League clubs must interview one candidate of color among an unlimited number of total interviews. After the interview, the club was free to proceed as it chose.

Mehri and Cochran could have taken a different approach. They could have urged that the League and its teams adopt a policy mandating that the teams consider racial diversity a plus in hiring head coaches. The University of Michigan Law School was at the time using such "plus factors" in admitting students, and the previous May the U.S. Court of Appeals for the Sixth Circuit had upheld the policy against legal challenge. While the Michigan case, *Grutter v. Bollinger*, involved public education rather than private employment, it was at least possible that the case would, if the U.S. Supreme Court chose to affirm it, support a similar policy in the NFL.

The Supreme Court had, without question, long viewed Title VII as condoning affirmative action in private employment hiring. Although the statute protects all employees, regardless of race, from employment discrimination, in the 1979 *United Steelworkers v. Weber* case the Court explained that the statute's prohibitions should be "read against the background of the legislative history of Title VII and the historical context from which the Act arose," a context indicating that the statute's chief purpose was to protect the employment opportunities of people of color. As such, when employers implemented affirmative action plans favoring members of traditionally underrepresented groups with the purpose of eliminating a "conspicuous" or "manifest" "racial imbalance," courts had supported them as long as the plans did not "unduly trammel the interests of majority group members." To guide lower courts' analyses, the Supreme Court, in the 1987 *Johnson v. Transportation Agency* case, offered insight as to when a plan might "trammel interests," indicating "interests might be trammeled if a plan required discharge of White workers for replacement by African American hires; was an 'absolute bar' to White employee advancement; or was a permanent, rather than a temporary, plan."

A temporary affirmative action plan utilizing "plus factors" for NFL head coach hiring, therefore, seemed a possibility under Title VII jurisprudence, even if the League and its teams were not instituting the plan to remedy any particular past discrimination. While a skeptic might argue that two restrictive post-*Johnson* Supreme Court decisions, *Richmond v. J. A. Croson Co.* and *Adarand Constructors, Inc. v. Pena*, would dampen that possibility (despite being decided under the Constitution's equal protection clause rather than under Title VII), the Michigan case would prove the perfect retort. If *Adarand* and *Croson*, both public contracting cases, impacted the private employment affirmative action context, then so, perhaps, should the *Grutter* case, which involved public education.

As it turned out, less than a year later the Supreme Court would uphold the University of Michigan's "plus factors" affirmative action plan. Moreover, the Court would detail, with reference to numerous private corporations' amicus arguments, the import of diverse perspectives not only in the classroom but in the workplace.

In 2002, however, even before the Supreme Court's *Grutter* decision, *Weber* and *Johnson* arguably provided the basis for a voluntary NFL affirmative action hiring program, and Mehri and Cochran could have pressed for just that. But they believed that if given a meaningful opportunity to compete for head coaching jobs, African American coaches would shine. An interview was all they asked; nothing more. Even so, commentator after commentator essentially accused Mehri and Cochran of attempting to forcibly install African Americans in head coaching positions across the League. Both Mehri and Cochran were accustomed to their intent being twisted, but it was nonetheless galling.

More absurd still were the attempted analogies between underrepresented African American coaches and underrepresented white players. Decades of documented discrimination had barred African Americans from NFL head coaching positions, and while the discrimination was no longer as obvious in its application, Madden's statistical analysis revealed that African American head coaching candidates continued to face discrimination. On the flip side, no evidence existed to suggest that white wide receivers, or any other white athletes for that matter, faced racially discriminatory barriers in their quest to play professional sports. To the contrary, if any athletes faced such discrimination, it was athletes of color.

Even after African Americans' proliferation and success in the nation's professional sports leagues, teams had attempted to limit African Americans' numbers on their rosters. The NBA's Boston Celtics franchise provides the paradigmatic example. Although the Celtics were the first team in the NBA to employ an African American player, to put an entirely African American team on the court at one time, and to hire an African American head coach, some twenty years after accomplishing those milestones—at a time when almost 75 percent of the NBA's players were African American—"the Celtics were conspicuous as the NBA team employing fewer African American players than any other. Indeed, during the 1985–86 and 1986–87 seasons, the Celtics' twelve-man roster consisted of four black players and eight white players and stood in sharp contrast with the composition of the league."

The team's composition was not coincidental. During the 1986–87 season, noting the Celtics' disproportionately high number of white players, University of Massachusetts sociologist Wornie Reed launched a statistical analysis of the disproportionality and concluded that the Celtics intentionally considered race in crafting the team's roster. That the 1985–86 and 1986–87 Celtics were exceptionally good teams does not defeat the conclusion. Rather, it suggests the *primary* contributors were meritoriously selected. "The Celtics' pattern," asserted Harvey Araton and Filip Bondy in their book *The Selling of the Green: The Financial Rise and Moral Decline of the Boston Celtics*, "is obvious: whenever they have had enough strength among their top eight players to contend for a championship, they have stacked the back end of their roster with token whites." The Celtics appeared so dedicated to this race-considered roster construction that disproportionate whiteness became central to the organization's identity. Even years after the Celtics abandoned such blatant discriminatory hiring practices, wrote *Washington Post* columnist and ESPN sports analyst Michael Wilbon, "the Celtics [were] synonymous with whiteness."

The Cleveland Cavaliers were similarly committed to ensuring a white presence on the team. Indeed, Cavs owner Ted Stepien once unabashedly declared, "[H]alf the squad should be white. I think people are afraid to speak out on that subject. . . . I'll be truthful, I respect [African Americans], but I need white people. It's in me." Although the Celtics and Cavs had by the end of the 1980s grown increasingly diverse, the Utah Jazz seemed to carry forward the tradition of considering race in constructing rosters. In fact, as of 2002, when Mehri and Cochran issued their report and Luke Smith wrote his column, the Jazz were in their twelfth consecutive year of fielding a team on which the percentage of white players outstripped the percentage of white players in the NBA at large.

While the racial animus that long motivated team and league management to bar African Americans from participating in America's premier sports leagues may well have contributed to this latter-day discrimination, economics proved the primary motivating force. Several academic studies, published over the course of many years, suggested that as sports developed during the latter half of the twentieth century into a substantial economic enterprise reliant on developing a fan base to pay admission and fill arena seats, team owners often concluded that attracting fans, and thus ensuring economic viability, demanded a substantial representation of white players.

Eleanor Brown, Diane Keenan, and Richard Spiro published perhaps the most thorough and damning such study in the *American Journal of Economics and Sociology* in 1991, just a few years after the Celtics compiled their grossly disproportionate rosters and at the start of the Jazz' decade-long run as the NBA's whitest team. The scholars' conclusion was blunt: white NBA fans, who vastly outnumber fans of other races at NBA games, "have a taste for seeing white players," and NBA teams have catered to that taste. They further concluded from their data that fans interested in seeing white players did not care whether the white players actually played in games as long as they were in uniform and sitting on the bench. The Celtics, it seemed, had already figured that out, as had much of the rest of the league: at the time, although 72.4 percent of the NBA's players were African American and 27.6 percent were white, among the league's infrequently used reserves only 47.4 percent were African American and 52.6 percent were white.

Although some researchers questioned the continued existence of racial considerations in roster construction, a 2002 *Journal of Sports Economics* study, reflecting back on the Brown, Keenan, and Spiro findings, concluded that more than a decade later, "[NBA] teams [were still] responding to customer discrimination." While perhaps most glaring in the NBA, the phenomenon's persistence was not restricted to that context, as revealed by a 2001 *Texas Hispanic Journal of Law and Policy* study concluding that, like the market for NBA players, "the market for Major League Baseball players is characterized by customer discrimination."

The NFL featured no documented, grievous team-wide racial disproportionalities, but it did feature one firmly established, long-standing realm of on-field white privilege: the quarterback position. The quarterback is generally his team's leader and chief tactician, and stereotypes of African American intellectual inferiority long presupposed African Americans incapable of effectively playing the position. Indeed, during the twenty-three seasons following the NFL's reintegration in 1946, the League featured only two African American quarterbacks, both of whom had short stints.

In 1969, though, James "Shack" Harris overcame the stereotypes, winning the Buffalo Bills' starting quarterback position as a rookie en route to a successful twelve-year NFL career. But Harris' success did little to alter NFL teams' approaches to staffing the quarterback position, and African American NFL quarterbacks remained a rarity. Doug Williams, despite quarterbacking the Washington Redskins to a 1988 Super Bowl victory and garnering Super Bowl Most Valuable Player honors in the process, was similarly unable to eradicate the myth that African Americans are poorly suited for the position.

Even as African Americans began quarterbacking high school teams in greater numbers, college scouts and coaches routinely insisted that they switch positions at the collegiate level. And those fortunate enough to play quarterback in college generally faced the same phenomenon when attempting to transition to the professional ranks. In fact, in the history of the NFL's annual college draft up until 1998, only three African American quarterbacks had been selected in the draft's first round, and even as the battle over equal coaching opportunity brewed in the NFL during the fall of 2002, despite African Americans constituting 65 percent of the League's players, they accounted for only 22 percent of the League's quarterbacks. To the extent some football players were, as Luke Smith put it, "being held to higher standards" on account of race, they were African Americans interested in playing quarterback, not whites interested in playing wide receiver.

Consistently challenging Smith's and others' assertions, however, required energy neither Mehri nor Cochran had. Winslow, who detested misinformation and who was, alongside Mehri, Cochran, and Wooten, by then donating a great deal of his time to pressing the NFL for equal coaching opportunity, occasionally issued counterpoints on the foursome's behalf, but he realized that the public debate had developed into a sideshow of sorts. The important conversations were occurring behind closed doors, and they were increasingly tending toward the foursome's view. Ultimately, as the NFL season entered its final stretch, with Rooney and Tagliabue leading the way, the owners' and executives' committees coalesced around the idea of diverse candidate slates. Once the committee's members reached agreement, the challenge became convincing the League's other owners as to the merits of their proposal, and once again Dan Rooney was out front. Some of his fellow owners were more amenable than others. Not every owner saw the NFL's lack of head coaching diversity as a problem, and some of those who did believed diverse candidate slates would be an inefficient and ineffective remedy. Despite this, Rooney pushed for unanimous agreement, and on the Friday before Christmas, he got it.

The Rooney Rule was born, but as time would quickly reveal, it was not without imperfections.

6

THE COACHING CAROUSEL

FRIDAY, DECEMBER 20, HAD BEEN A WHIRLWIND, and the following morning Mehri was still trying to figure it all out. At 5:00 p.m. on Friday, the *Washington Post*'s NFL correspondent, Len Shapiro, who had tracked Mehri and Cochran's efforts more closely than any other journalist in the country, called Mehri to announce that the NFL owners had just unanimously agreed to utilize diverse candidate slates when seeking to fill head coaching vacancies. Ever the wary lawyer, Mehri, rather than exulting, dissected Shapiro's news, and immediately grew concerned.

First, the owners, it turned out, had agreed via handshake rather than contract or anything of the like. Only their collective word bound them, and Mehri, not knowing the owners, had no idea what their collective word was worth. Furthermore, their agreement was short on details. They had committed neither to a process by which they would interview candidates nor to the nature of those interviews. Mehri did not believe the League should micromanage each club's interviewing approach, but he believed minimum standards were necessary to avoid farcical interviews. In addition, Mehri wished the owners had established an enforcement mechanism in the event one among them disregarded the agreement. Cochran agreed with Mehri's instincts, and the two worked into the night to draft a joint press statement commending the NFL and its owners but registering their concerns about implementation and enforcement.

Mehri awoke on Saturday morning as conflicted as he had been after finally issuing the press statement the previous night, and as he set out to the local Whole Foods Market to begin his weekly grocery run, he continued to speculate as to what the handshake agreement really meant. In the store's produce section, as Mehri looked over the fresh vegetable options, he got his answer.

Retrieving his ringing cell phone from his pocket, Mehri saw Wooten's number flash across the digital display and, wondering what Wooten's take on Friday's news would be, he raised the phone to his ear. Mehri had hardly greeted his friend before Wooten blurted out: "Cyrus, you came out of nowhere and changed the NFL." The statement took Mehri aback. He viewed the owners' agreement as a mildly positive development, but Wooten clearly viewed it more enthusiastically. Wooten's perspective benefited from history. While not perfect, the owners' agreement represented the strongest commitment to equal opportunity he had ever seen the League make.

For thirty minutes, standing among the vegetables and the shoppers sorting through them, Mehri chatted with Wooten, and by the time Mehri returned his phone to his pocket, he was convinced they had prevailed; in fact, he grew a bit giddy thinking about how quickly it had all happened. When he and Cochran had initially released their report and engaged the NFL in discussions, they'd done so with an eye toward immediate impact. They were uninterested in several years' worth of focus group sessions and exploratory committees. The League's African American coaches had waited long enough for a fair shake, and he and Cochran had set out to ensure they would receive just that when the League's teams next hired head coaches. Wooten believed the agreement was evidence they had achieved their goal, and Mehri began to believe the same.

Grocery shopping had never been more fun. Overwhelmed with their accomplishment, Mehri walked the Whole Foods aisles thinking far more about the impending annual NFL coaching carousel than about his grocery list. Mehri was certain that if black coaches were given equal opportunity, which the owners had at least ostensibly promised to provide, the nation would soon see a more diverse NFL head coaching corps. As Mehri paid for his goods, packed them in his car, and headed home, he recalled the promise he had made to Bryant Gumbel just three months earlier: that the NFL would change. Now it apparently had.

It was a good feeling, and it lasted for almost four hours.

THE DALLAS COWBOYS were the team of the 1990s, winning three Super Bowls that decade to add to the two they had won many years earlier. With an explosive offense and a charismatic swagger, "America's Team" truly captivated the nation. By 2002, though, their offense was anemic, their swagger was gone, and they had not won a playoff game in six years. They were terrible, which was completely unacceptable to their owner, Jerry Jones.

Jones, a wealthy gas and oil magnate, was accustomed to success and unafraid to make abrupt personnel changes to achieve it. When he purchased the Cowboys in 1989, after the team suffered an embarrassing thirteen-loss season, he immediately and unceremoniously fired Tom Landry, the only head coach in the Cowboys' twenty-nine-year history. Shortly thereafter he forced Tex Schramm, the team's longtime general manager, out of the organization, and he hired Jimmy Johnson, the former University of Miami head football coach, to fill both roles. Despite Super Bowl victories in 1993 and 1994, Jones was dissatisfied with Johnson and fired him, reportedly proclaiming, "There were 500 coaches who could have won the Super Bowl" with the talented Cowboys roster. Jones then installed former University of Oklahoma head football coach Barry Switzer as the Cowboys' head coach and began acting as his own general manager.

Switzer captured a third Super Bowl for Jones, but after four years at the helm, Switzer was gone in favor of Chan Gailey, the Pittsburgh Steelers' former offensive coordinator. Gailey took the

Cowboys to the playoffs twice in two years, but he did not win a playoff game, and Jones quickly replaced him with Dave Campo.

When Campo took over in 2000, he promised to restore the Cowboys' pride in the new millennium. After two 5–11 seasons, however, it was a wonder he still had a job. Johnson, Switzer, and Gailey all won more games than they lost and took the Cowboys to the playoffs multiple times, and Johnson and Switzer both won Super Bowls. Notwithstanding those accomplishments, Jones had fired them all. So, at 10–22 over two seasons, Campo began the 2002 campaign on borrowed time, and he knew it.

At the season's inception, in hopes of changing the team's fortunes, Campo promoted a hard-nosed, blue-collar mentality. He drilled his philosophy into his players by, among other things, insisting they punch a time clock when arriving at work. He wanted them to envision themselves as laborers toiling together to build a house, and he wanted them to view their season as that house. He expected a completed abode by season's end, with the top floor representing the playoffs.

If the Cowboys' season was indeed a house, then construction was flawed from the start. In the season opener, the Cowboys played the Houston Texans, an expansion team playing its first-ever NFL game. In four decades, no expansion team had won its inaugural game, and the Cowboys were favored to win by more than a touchdown. Still, the Cowboys found a way to lose, and the loss set the tone for the season. Halfway through the season's sixteen games, the Cowboys had won only three of their eight contests, and *Dallas Morning News* reporter Chip Brown advised that their metaphorical house be examined for toxic mold.

Six games later, by mid-December, they were worse still, nursing a 5–9 record and fresh off the heels of a 37–7 pounding at the hands of division rival New York Giants. It was the most lopsided loss of Campo's head coaching career, and even though two games remained in the season, Campo's ouster was a virtual certainty. The only open questions, both of which sparked intense speculation throughout the NFL community, were when Jones would fire Campo and whom Jones would appoint to succeed him. On Saturday, December 21, just a few hours after Mehri returned from his grocery run, CBS broadcast the seeming answers: very soon and Bill Parcells.

At the time, Parcells was an ESPN analyst, but during the previous twenty years he had established himself as a Hall of Fame–caliber head coach, winning two Super Bowls with the New York Giants and also achieving substantial success with the New England Patriots and New York Jets.

With all three organizations, Parcells inherited weak teams and molded them into winners. The Giants were emerging from a losing season in 1982 when Parcells replaced Ray Perkins as the team's head coach. Two years later, they ended the season 9–7. Two years after that, they won Super Bowl XXI, and four years later, in 1990, they won a second Super Bowl, after which Parcells retired from coaching. In 1993, however, Parcells decided to coach again when offered the New England Patriots' head coaching position. The Patriots were a lowly 2–14 the season before Parcells' arrival, but with Parcells in charge, they rapidly improved, and during the 1996 season they won the AFC Championship. Unfortunately for Patriots fans, Parcells and Patriots owner Bob Kraft had difficulty coexisting, and Parcells left after that season to coach the pathetic New York Jets.

While Parcells' 1996 Patriots were marching through the playoffs, the Jets, having suffered through a painful 1–15 season, were at home watching. As he had done twice before, Parcells quickly transformed his new club's fortunes, and during the 1998 season he led the Jets to the AFC Championship.

Although Parcells retired again after the 1999 season, he remained arguably the nation's best-known and most effective coach, and after leaving the game, he burned to return to the sidelines. His desire to reenter the NFL appeared to peak in 2002. In January of that year, Parcells expressed intense interest in the Tampa Bay Buccaneers' head coaching job and, in fact, signed an employment contract with the Bucs before backing out at the last moment. And in early December Parcells reportedly asked a third party to explore with the

University of Alabama a potential head coaching post there. Parcells was at bottom a football guy, and he seemed lost without the sport.

As much as he loved to coach, the work emotionally taxed him, and he had developed a reputation, as exhibited with the Bucs, for flirting with teams but then opting for continued retirement. Parcells had, according to *Washington Post* columnist and ESPN sports analyst Tony Kornheiser, "left more suitors at the altar than Julia Roberts in 'Runaway Bride.'"

In late 2002, though, Parcells' love for the game was not the only force motivating his renewed interest in prowling the sidelines. Parcells had apparently just endured a financially messy divorce and had overextended his resources in buying thoroughbred racehorses. It seemed he needed money, and he knew he could make plenty as a coach. Whatever Parcells' primary impetus, with his coaching track record he appeared an attractive hire for any team, including, evidently, the Cowboys.

According to the CBS report, earlier in the week Jones flew in his private jet to Teterboro Airport in Teterboro, New Jersey, not far from Parcells' home. Parcells reportedly met Jones at the airport and the two talked for three hours in one of the terminal's private rooms. Thereafter they adjourned to Jones' plane, where they spoke for an additional two hours. For several days their five-hour summit remained a secret, but it eventually leaked, and once it did, media outlets across the country seized on the story: the NFL's highest-profile team seemed poised to hire professional football's most renowned coach.

Amid the media clamor, both Jones and Parcells denied their meeting was anything more than a friendly chat. "We didn't talk about the job of coaching the Dallas Cowboys," Jones stated when pressed. "We just had general talks about football and the NFL." Parcells issued a similar statement, insisting they "discussed pro football, philosophy and the Cowboys," but not the prospect of Parcells coaching the team.

For many, the denials rang hollow. Although Jones had publicly stated he would wait until season's end to evaluate Campo, sources close to both Parcells and Jones were reporting that Jones had already decided Campo was done in Dallas and that Jones had traveled to New Jersey specifically to assess Parcells' interest in coaching the Cowboys. Parcells himself admitted that during their discussion Jones queried him about his willingness to resume coaching, but only casually. The sources, however, indicated the discussion had gone much further than either Jones or Parcells would acknowledge, with the two ultimately discussing a prospective salary of roughly $3 million per season.

Any number of reasons might have motivated Jones' and Parcells' desire for secrecy and, once the story broke, their apparent deception. Perhaps Jones sought to spare Campo the humiliation of following his replacement's courtship in the press. Perhaps Parcells didn't want to frighten away other potential suitors with the news that he was in talks with the Cowboys. Perhaps Jones and Parcells simply viewed the conversation as their business; after all, NFL owners had been interviewing and hiring coaches on their own terms without substantive League oversight since the League's founding.

In light of the NFL's new equal opportunity initiative, of course, there existed another potential explanation. Perhaps Jones was seeking to shield himself from public scrutiny under the Rooney Rule. If indeed Jones had flown to New Jersey to recruit Parcells to become his head coach and to discuss deal terms, he had grossly undermined the rule's purpose. The rule, which the owners had been discussing for some time, and to which Jones would formally agree just two days after returning from New Jersey, existed precisely to prevent the singular focus such a meeting would reflect. Through the rule, the NFL sought to broaden the pool of head coaching candidates to include those who might otherwise be overlooked because of race, and a headlong pursuit of Parcells would clearly contravene that goal. Under such circumstances, the *Washington Post*'s Leonard Shapiro observed, "[a]ny other interview with a minority candidate before an official announcement of a Parcells hiring would have to be considered meaningless."

Whether Jones orchestrated his meeting with Parcells to avoid Rooney Rule–related criticism or for other reasons, once word of the meeting surfaced, Jones' subsequent actions challenged the rule's very foundation. He engaged Parcells in a "whirlwind two-week courtship," which involved a second flight to the East Coast, this one to New York, where the two met at a Garden City, Long Island, hotel for a long discussion. All told, Jones met face-to-face with Parcells for roughly eleven hours. At some point during the courtship, Jones stole thirty minutes to telephonically interview former Minnesota Vikings head coach Dennis Green, an African American, before returning his attention to Parcells. Green's was the "meaningless" interview about which Shapiro had warned, and he was obviously never a bona fide candidate.

As discussions between Jones and Parcells intensified during the holiday season, Mehri and Cochran grew increasingly agitated, and they railed through the press against the Cowboys' impropriety.

"What's happened in Dallas has all the hallmarks of the old hiring practices instead of what the NFL said it was going to do," Mehri stormed when asked for comment. "Jones is flying off to New Jersey and Long Island to meet with Parcells without giving a minority candidate a fair shot. It looks like the old regime, not a new day."

Mehri chafed at Jones' apparent intellectual dishonesty. Jones, he insisted, knew precisely why the Rooney Rule existed, and it wasn't to provide token interviews. It was to provide genuine opportunity. The rule, as Jones applied it, was worthless. Indeed, it was worse than no rule at all. It made a mockery of Green's candidacy.

Jones, uninterested in a public tussle and obviously confident that the Green interview satisfied his obligation, said little in response. The League, for its part, was even less forthcoming: it issued no public comment on the Cowboys' process, creating the impression of disinterest in the developing controversy. In actuality, the League was deeply concerned, and Goodell himself had spoken with Jones about the importance of a truly inclusive process. As Goodell would later explain, it was obvious the Cowboys had "locked onto Bill Parcells. They had a chance to get somebody like a Parcells and they said, 'That's the guy I want.'" If Green stood a chance, in Goodell's view it wasn't a strong one.

Still, Goodell and others at 280 Park Avenue believed, for several reasons, that the League would be on shaky ground in sanctioning Jones. First, despite the transparency of Jones' desire for Parcells, the Cowboys' owner had fulfilled, in fact if not in spirit, the policy's requirement of interviewing one candidate of color. Second, Green never complained that Jones had simply used him to satisfy the rule. Had Green publicly or even confidentially expressed bitterness, it likely would have changed the dynamic, but since Green had indicated he was comfortable with the interview he received, the League was reluctant to characterize it as a sham. Finally, penalizing Jones for his technically compliant process, some of which occurred before the rule was formally adopted, risked disgruntling other owners and threatening the unanimous agreement the rule enjoyed. The League's top officials were not thrilled, but neither were they prepared to act.

"If you were making the decisions yourself, you wouldn't necessarily have wanted the Cowboys' search to be the first thing that happened," Pash later acknowledged, reflecting on the League's tenuous position, "but it was one of those cases where you say, 'Let's not overreact. We're early in the hiring process. We're early in the hiring season. Let's see what happens, and then let's make an assessment.'"

Mehri and Cochran, unaware of the NFL's ruminations but aware of its inaction, expressed displeasure to whomever would listen, and while they continued to assert their commitment to avoid litigation, they promised they were not "ruling anything out" in their quest to reform the NFL. Three months earlier, their public litigation threat and the media maelstrom it created had helped spur the NFL into discussions and ultimately spawned the Rooney Rule. This time, though, it did nothing. Jones did not modify his search process, the League did not step in, and on January 2, 2003, what for weeks had seemed inevitable came to pass: Parcells became the head coach of the Dallas Cowboys.

The Rooney Rule, for which so many had worked so feverishly over the course of the previous several months, suddenly seemed like a joke, and with the NFL unwilling to punish the Cowboys, Mehri and Cochran hoped the owners still searching for head coaches would take the rule more seriously than Jones had.

The Cincinnati Bengals, by all accounts the League's worst team, were next to launch a head coach search. The Bengals had never been one of the NFL's premier franchises, and although they appeared in two Super Bowls during the 1980s, they had subsequently steadily declined. Since 1990, the Bengals' last winning season, they had been not just subpar but abysmal, with the last few years their most horrendous. Head coach Dick LeBeau, who three winless games into the 2000 season took over for Bruce Coslet, captained the Bengals to an embarrassing .267 winning percentage during his almost three years at the helm and culminated his tenure in 2002 with a 2–14 record. Although LeBeau had been an effective defensive coordinator with both the Steelers and the Bengals, his success as a coordinator did not translate into head coaching success. Indeed, both his overall winning percentage as a head coach and the team's 2002 campaign set records for franchise futility.

The numbers alone did not fully reflect the Bengals' struggles. The franchise had stagnated over the years. As other teams expanded their scouting operations and modernized their facilities, the Bengals largely maintained the status quo, and few in professional football wanted anything to do with the organization. Indeed, players the League over viewed the Bengals as an "antiquated and doddering" mess—"the Flintstones of the NFL," as one former Bengal put it. Those drafted or acquired through trades by the Bengals were for the most part displeased, and their free agent comrades, given their druthers, generally looked elsewhere for employment.

If ever a team needed a new direction—a new approach to hiring as well as to its other operations—it was the 2002 Cincinnati Bengals. Still, when Bengals owner Mike Brown, speaking of the Rooney Rule at the beginning of his head coach search, publicly stated, "This is the policy, and we will comply," there was little reason to believe his definition of compliance would differ much from Jones'. After all, the Bengals were, in Mehri's words, the "poster child" for everything the Rooney Rule stood against. In the Bengals' thirty-five-year history, they had never hired a head coach, offensive coordinator, or defensive coordinator of color. Indeed, they had never even interviewed a person of color for any of those positions. And although the Bengals' coaching staff, which featured four coaches of color, was only marginally less diverse than the average NFL coaching staff, the historical homogeneity in the coaching staff's upper echelons suggested that none of the four would ever receive a substantial promotion. If such a promotion had been possible, it seemed, running backs coach Jim Anderson certainly would have received one by then.

Over the course of eighteen years, Anderson coached four Bengals running backs to eight Pro Bowl seasons. No other Bengals position coach had come close to eliciting such consistent success from his players. Moreover, in ten of those eighteen years, the Bengals finished the season among the League's top ten rushing teams, twice finishing first. Nevertheless, even though the Bengals had not posted a winning season for twelve consecutive years and had changed head coaches three times during that span, the team had never granted Anderson an interview for its offensive coordinator position, much less its head coaching position.

The ranks of those with power in the organization's front office were similarly "lily-white." In fact, the team's staff directory, which was sixty-five names long, included just two people of color. One, Jason Williams, was a ticket office employee. The other, former Bengals running back Eric Ball, was the director of player relations, a job that involves interacting and communicating with the team's players but rarely allows any real authority. It was the one director-level front office role NFL teams routinely entrusted to African Americans.

The Bengals' history and minimally diverse organizational structure did not bode well for the Rooney Rule's prospects, and neither did the Bengals' location, which was not exactly a bastion of progressive pluralism. Situated just across the Ohio River from rural Kentucky, Cincinnati had long been among the nation's most racially discordant cities and in recent times had been virtually unrivaled in that respect. During the previous several years, Cincinnati police officers had killed fourteen African American men, and relations between the city's police department and its African American community had grown increasingly icy and brittle. Members of the African American community viewed the killings as the natural outgrowth of officers' consistently intimidating and harassing presence in their neighborhoods. In their view, members of their community were police targets and racial profiling was an everyday occurrence.

The numbers seemed to bear out their concerns. A study of 141,000 traffic tickets issued over the course of almost two years by Cincinnati police revealed that although African Americans accounted for only 37.5 percent of Cincinnati's residents, officers cited four times as many African Americans as whites for driving without proof of insurance and twice as many African Americans as whites for both driving without a license and driving without a seatbelt. Such secondary violations are identifiable only after a motorist is pulled over for some other reason, and the statistics were therefore highly suggestive of profiling. Nevertheless, police largely denied the bias allegations. Moreover, with regard to the fatal shootings, they asserted that the officers' actions were both non-race-related and justified under the circumstances, noting that the majority of the fourteen men were armed when killed.

The community was unconvinced, however, and on March 14, 2001, a group of African American citizens, represented by longtime Cincinnati lawyer Al Gerhardstein, filed a federal racial discrimination lawsuit against the Cincinnati Police Department. With little meaningful dialogue, positions and perspectives grew entrenched, distrust reigned, and it appeared an ugly legal battle was in the making.

On April 8, 2001, it became clear the brewing hostility would not be contained in the courtroom. At 2:00 a.m. a nineteen-year-old African American man, Timothy Thomas, was walking outside a nightclub in Over-the-Rhine, one of Cincinnati's underresourced, predominantly African American neighborhoods. A police officer approached him, and he ran. Within seconds, the police radio was blaring, describing Thomas and tracking his route: "Ah we have a suspect, male, black, about 6 foot, red bandana, last seen east bound on east 13th. He has, ah, about 14 warrants on him." Additional officers responded, and Thomas was suddenly the target of a man-hunt.

The officers had no reason to know, and the dispatcher did not explain, that the warrants were relatively harmless, as far as warrants go. Indeed, Thomas had never committed a serious crime in his life. The warrants resulted from nonmoving secondary traffic violations. Moreover, the officers likely could not have known that most of the warrants had accrued over the course of just two months, during which ten officers pulled Thomas over a total of eleven times and issued him twenty-one tickets. Without such knowledge, they could not have considered, even if inclined to, the possibility that Thomas was a racial profiling victim who had grown to so dread police encounters that he chose that night to flee into the seeming safety of darkness. So when Officer Stephen Roach spotted Thomas in an empty alley and thought he saw Thomas reach into his pants for a gun, Roach fired.

Two years earlier and hundreds of miles away in the South Bronx, a similar scene had unfolded at a similar time of night. Four officers witnessed a black man standing on his apartment building's stoop. Taking him for either a burglary lookout or a serial rapist, they approached him, and the man hastily retreated into the building's vestibule. Officer Sean Carroll, believing the man was reaching for a gun, began to shoot. Forty-one shots later, Amadou Diallo, who moments earlier had simply walked out to his stoop for a breath of fresh air and who was brandishing only a wallet, was dead, killed because of color and context.

Psychologist Keith Payne, motivated by the Diallo tragedy, designed an experiment in hopes of deconstructing what had happened that night in the Bronx. Payne asked white Americans to watch a computer screen on which he flashed a picture of either a black face or a white face and then flashed a picture of either a gun or a hand tool, such as a wrench or a drill. Asked to identify the object, those initially shown a black face were quicker to identify the gun as a gun. When Payne sped up the experiment, demanding that the subjects return a verdict within a half second of seeing the object, blackness and the gun correlated even more strongly. Under such pressure, subjects initially shown a black face were quicker to identify the gun as a gun, but also quicker to identify the hand tool as a gun.

Nothing Payne told the subjects beforehand, not even a thorough explanation of the experiment coupled with a plea that they avoid drawing on any racial stereotypes, impacted outcomes. The only way to reduce the bias was to give subjects more time to identify the object. "When we make a split-second decision," Payne explained, "we are really vulnerable to being guided by our stereotypes and prejudices, even ones we may not necessarily endorse or believe."

Diallo's wallet, concluded author Malcolm Gladwell, who explored Payne's study in his bestselling book *Blink: The Power of Thinking Without Thinking*, was no different from Payne's hand tool: "Diallo is black, and it's late, and it's the South Bronx, and time is being measured now in milliseconds, and under those circumstances we know that wallets invariably look like guns."

Late at night in Over-the-Rhine, alone in an alley with Thomas, Roach thought he saw what Carroll had thought he'd seen. But there was no gun, just a scared African American young man trying to pull up his oversized pants. Roach fired, and an hour later, Thomas was dead. Less than twenty-four hours after that, Cincinnati was burning. The tension blanketing the city for years had given way to war.

African Americans, racked with grief and anger, attacked police stations, businesses, and municipal infrastructure, and police countered with rubber bullets, pepper spray, and batons. For nearly a week, a sickening, cyclical battle raged. Daylight hours were relatively calm, but come dark of night, the violence erupted again. And with each night, injuries and arrests mounted. Cincinnati had experienced nothing of the sort since the 1960s civil rights movement. Frightened residents sequestered themselves in their homes, and out-of-towners steered clear of the city. Before long, the national media descended, broadcasting Cincinnati's woes to the world and prompting Great Britain to issue a travel advisory to its citizens planning trips to the area.

Desperate for peace, Mayor Charlie Luken ultimately declared a citywide curfew from 8:00 p.m. through 6:00 a.m., and the uprising began to ebb. The tension, however, did not. Cincinnati's African American community felt as disenfranchised and under siege as it had a week earlier, and initiated a series of protests. A general boycott of Cincinnati quickly took root, with celebrities and noncelebrities alike choosing not to patronize the city. In the year following the unrest, Whoopi Goldberg canceled a performance in the city. Bill Cosby and Smokey Robinson did the same. In addition, one of the city's summer jewels, the annual Cincinnati Jazz Festival, which had for forty years attracted tens of thousands of spectators from throughout the Midwest and South, failed to enroll a corporate sponsor and, with musicians' boycotts imminent, was canceled.

Although the city, as a part of the agreement settling the lawsuit filed three weeks before Thomas' death, agreed to implement broad-based community policing reforms and took several other steps to heal its racial wounds, at the end of 2002, when it became clear the Bengals would be shopping for a new head coach, the boycott endured and Cincinnati continued to struggle with racial tension.

At the mercy of a team that had never previously considered a person of color for its head coaching position and which was based in a racial powder keg of a city, the Rooney Rule's future looked bleak. Rooney Rule supporters might be able to dismiss one failure, which the Cowboys' search clearly was, as aberrant. But if the Bengals granted a lone candidate of color a meaningless interview during an otherwise thorough search, it would create a nascent pattern of Rooney Rule end-arounds. Assuming the NFL did not object, which seemed a reasonably safe assumption in light of the League's silence during the Cowboys' search, the end-around might well become standard operating procedure for NFL teams looking for a head coach. If so, the Rooney Rule would be impotent—just another well-intentioned but ineffective attempt to change the NFL's culture.

But Mike Brown did precisely what he'd promised to do. He complied with the rule, executing a search of the sort Mehri and Cochran might have designed were they NFL owners. In six days, Brown interviewed five candidates. Three—Bengals defensive coordinator Mark Duffner, Pittsburgh Steelers offensive coordinator Mike Mularkey, and recently deposed Jacksonville Jaguars head coach Tom Coughlin—were white. Two—the long-overlooked Bengals running backs coach Jim Anderson and Washington Redskins defensive coordinator Marvin Lewis—were African American. Each received a serious, substantive, face-to-face meeting worthy of an equal employment opportunity best-practices manual.

In just a few days, Brown had discharged his duty under the rule. Going forward, he was free to handle his search as he wanted. If he chose to grant the white candidates subsequent interviews and cast the African American candidates aside, under the rule he was free to do so. Or if he chose to simply end the search and hire one of the white candidates with no further process, he could have done that. The Rooney Rule no longer bore on Brown's hiring process, which, if the rumor mill swirling before the Bengals' search was to be believed, meant Tom Coughlin would be the next head coach of the Bengals.

From the beginning, Tom Coughlin had been the odds-on favorite. He was a fine coach who had led the Jaguars to a respectable 68–60 record over eight years. In addition, he was a firm disciplinarian renowned throughout the League as a no-nonsense taskmaster, and the Bengals, by most estimates, needed just that. Under LeBeau, a reputed players' coach, the Bengals performed poorly. Coughlin seemed the perfect antidote.

Brown, however, resisted a reflexive Coughlin coronation. He deliberated in all the ways Jones had not when pursuing Parcells, and in the end Brown's deliberation paid off handsomely. It familiarized him with Marvin Lewis.

On some level, of course, Brown, like everyone in the League with a pulse, knew about Lewis and what he could do. Lewis' body of work as an assistant coach in the NFL over the course of a decade, and in particular his success with the 2000 Baltimore Ravens' record-shattering and Super Bowl–winning defensive unit, testified to that. And although some in the football world called Lewis a genius, he was certainly not a mad or mean one. He was a grounded, hardworking straight shooter, both polite and friendly but not ostentatiously so—the type of guy whom, were he your neighbor, you would ask to keep your spare house key. That is, of course, unless his race concerned you, in which case you might be hesitant to trust him with your keys, or for that matter, with your football franchise.

Although six NFL teams sought head coaches after Lewis' legendary season, he received nary an offer and only one interview, the sincerity and substance of which Lewis' agent publicly questioned. It was true that under NFL rules a coach could not interview for head coaching positions with other teams until that coach's season was complete, but the best assistant coaches, even those whose teams played in the Super Bowl, routinely had suitors waiting. Only one ostensibly interested team was willing to wait for Lewis. The racial dynamics involved in Lewis' snubbing, at least in the view of African Americans throughout the League, could not be ignored.

"It's just difficult to imagine," Tony Dungy explained at the time, speaking, it seemed, for an entire community. "You would have thought more than one team out of the [six] would say that here's a guy that should be at least talked to. And you can only beg the question in your mind: If he were white, would it have been one out of [six]? I don't think so." The following season, Lewis' defense was again outstanding, yet again he received no offers, strengthening the sense that, as Michael Wilbon put it, "most NFL owners would rather buy stock in recently bankrupt United Airlines than hire a black head coach."

If Mike Brown had been one of the NFL owners Wilbon had been thinking of before the sit-down with Lewis, Brown had left that camp by meeting's end. By all accounts the coach wowed Brown, and many commentators, upon learning of Brown's impressions, began citing Lewis, rather than Coughlin, as the man to beat. Coughlin, however, remained an attractive potential hire, and after the Bengals interviewed each of the five candidates, Lewis and Coughlin led the pack.

Within a week, the team had interviewed both coaches for a second time, and it became clear one of the two would soon be named the Bengals' next head coach. The question was which one. The Bengals' principal decision makers all liked both Lewis and Coughlin, but Brown reportedly favored Coughlin, while executive vice president Katie Blackburn, Brown's daughter and heir apparent, reportedly favored Lewis.

Ultimately, Coughlin, who had been the general manager as well as the head coach in Jacksonville, seemed to cool on the prospect of joining the Bengals once it became obvious the job would entail, at best, a managerial power share with Brown. Lewis, on the other hand, had grown increasingly enthusiastic about the position, which seemed to intensify the Bengals' enthusiasm about Lewis, and on January 14, just a few days after the second interviews, Bengals executives made their decision and were trying desperately to track Lewis down. Although the Bengals' officials and Lewis were all in suburban Alabama that morning for the Senior Bowl, a college all-star game that coaches and front office personnel across the League assiduously scout, they could not reach Lewis on his cell phone.

Finally Katie Blackburn and her husband, Troy, the team's director of business development, anxious to get their offer on the table, set out on foot to search the hotel in which Lewis was staying. They eventually found Lewis and learned his radio silence was the consequence of clumsiness rather than cold feet—he had accidentally dropped his phone in his hotel room toilet, rendering it inoperable. By midday Lewis and the Bengals had agreed to terms, and that evening, in the Lagoon Room of the Marriott Grand in Point Clear, Alabama, Mike Brown introduced Lewis, the first African American the Bengals had ever interviewed for one of its top coaching positions, as the team's next head coach.

The Bengals' hire meant that only one NFL team, the Jacksonville Jaguars, was still looking for a coach, and the Jaguars' search, which had already dragged on for over two weeks, was grinding to its conclusion with the Carolina Panthers' defensive coordinator, Jack Del Rio, as the presumptive favorite for the job. From Mehri and

Cochran's perspective, the Jaguars' search was suboptimal but not as galling as the Cowboys' search had been. The search was odd in that Jaguars owner Wayne Weaver had initially articulated a preference for an offensive-minded head coach, which seemed to disqualify Lewis and renowned New York Jets defensive coordinator Ted Cottrell, two of the strongest African American candidates in the head coaching pool. Notwithstanding that expressed preference, the Jaguars seemed to be settling on Del Rio, a defensive coach who had been one of Lewis' subordinates in Baltimore. If the job description had changed such that Del Rio became a candidate, Rooney Rule supporters grumbled, Lewis and Cottrell should have been invited to interview as well.

But there was no evidence that Weaver had homed in on Del Rio to the exclusion of other candidates, as Jones had homed in on Parcells. Indeed, if Dennis Green, whom the Jaguars did interview, had been willing to serve as the Jaguars' head coach without any general manager duties, he likely would have been a strong contender. Green, however, had previously established himself as a successful NFL head coach and wanted greater institutional control, which Weaver was unwilling to grant.

From an equal opportunity perspective, most Rooney Rule supporters viewed the Jaguars' soon-to-conclude search as falling somewhere between the Cowboys' and the Bengals' searches: it was neither a disgraceful process nor an ideal one, and although the search was disappointing, on balance the Rooney Rule looked as if it would emerge from the coaching carousel bruised but unbowed.

Then, just a day after the Bengals hired Lewis, the San Francisco 49ers, in the surprise firing of the year, terminated their head coach, Steve Mariucci. The 49ers were coming off a playoff season (although the Tampa Bay Buccaneers had just battered them 31–6, ending their Super Bowl hopes) and Mariucci had done well during his six years as the 49ers' head coach. But his relationship with team management had never been strong, and tensions had recently risen over divergent views as to the organization's direction. Team owner John York didn't say much about his reasons, just that there existed "a difference in philosophy within the 49ers' structure on how best to utilize our various talents." With that, Mariucci, known widely as "Mooch," was done in San Francisco.

Mariucci's firing spawned two direct consequences, one obvious and the other less so. The first was that the 49ers would soon be hiring a new head coach. The second was that the Detroit Lions would do likewise. The 49ers' selection would eventually emerge from a long search that satisfied the Rooney Rule. The Lions' selection was a foregone conclusion: Mooch.

7

MILLEN, MOOCH, AND THE GREAT
DETROIT HIRING DEBATE

IN LATE DECEMBER, the Lions had quieted rumors that they might fire their head coach, Marty Mornhinweg. Although Mornhinweg had performed poorly during his two-year tenure, compiling a 5–27 record and losing all sixteen of the Lions' road games, the team's general manager, Matt Millen, resolutely announced the team was retaining him: "The same reasons that I hired him still exist, and we move forward." Four weeks later, in late January, Millen was just as resolute in jettisoning Mornhinweg: "Earlier this afternoon I let Coach Mornhinweg go, for a number of reasons. It was something we felt we had to do, and we move forward."

Millen declined to elaborate on the reasons for Mornhinweg's firing, which was just as well. Nothing he could have said would have obscured the obvious: Millen wanted Mariucci.

"Of all the sham news conferences I have ever attended," wrote *Detroit Free Press* columnist Michael Rosenberg, "Millen's was the most sham-ful. Everybody in the room knew he fired Mornhinweg because Mariucci was available. They knew it in Allen Park [Michigan], they knew it in San Francisco, they knew it in Tokyo."

They all knew it because Millen had been salivating over Mariucci for years. In 1998, when Lions owner William Clay Ford Sr. first contemplated hiring Millen as the Lions' general manager, Millen was apparently poised to pursue Mariucci as his head coach. Ford opted against hiring Millen at that point, but when he hired him three years later, in 2001, Millen predictably sought out Mariucci. At that point Mariucci was committed to the 49ers, so Millen hired Mariucci's offensive coordinator, Mornhinweg, instead. Millen propositioned Mariucci again toward the end of the 2002 regular season, but Mariucci declined, secure in the belief the 49ers would retain him for the remainder of his contract and potentially grant him a contract extension. When the 49ers fired Mariucci several weeks later, however, Millen saw his opportunity and fired Mornhinweg to clear the decks.

Although transparently obsessive and myopic, Millen's Mariucci quest was rationally rooted. Mariucci was a good coach and a good friend, someone to whom Millen was willing to entrust his career. In just three years as a general manager, Millen, whose prior NFL experience consisted solely of playing and network broadcasting, had mismanaged his way into the ranks of the League's all-time worst executives. He was fortunate to still be employed, and he knew that if his new hire failed, he likely would be out of a job. Mariucci, he hoped, would be his savior.

Just as everyone from Allen Park to San Francisco to Tokyo knew Millen was going to hire Mariucci, so too did everyone in the NFL, including the League's African American head coaching candidates. And none of them wanted to be to the Lions what Green had been just a month earlier to the Cowboys: a token. Enduring an interview that likely would be fruitless but held a glimmer of promise was one thing. Signing up for inevitable rejection was quite another, and as fastidiously as Millen tried to entice a candidate of color to interview for the job, nobody bit. First Green politely declined; then Pittsburgh Steelers defensive coordinator Tim Lewis did the same. As the rejections mounted, it became increasingly clear that Detroit would be ground zero for the Rooney Rule battle, and when Millen finally abandoned his search for an interviewee of color and hired Mariucci, it was certain. Whereas Jones had violated the Rooney Rule's spirit, Millen and the Lions, by not interviewing a candidate of color, had violated its letter. This was the test case that would make or break the rule.

Millen, knowing the fight was imminent, immediately took the offensive. Even before introducing Mariucci at a press conference called for that purpose on February 4, 2003, Millen spoke of the NFL's "process" and emphasized the Lions' commitment to it. He said little more on the topic, but the mere mention during an otherwise celebratory press conference spoke volumes. Millen wanted the record to reflect that he knew about the Rooney Rule, had attempted to discharge his duty under it, and had failed to do so not out of ignorance or disdain but due to circumstances beyond his control. His core message, albeit unspoken, was simple: he had not refused to interview candidates of color; they had refused him.

A number of NFL reporters were sympathetic to his plight: what was Millen to do if nobody would interview? He could not force them, and if they chose not to interview, the fault was obviously theirs, not his. Others reporters countered that the fault was clearly his, not theirs. Millen's refusal from the outset to consider options other than Mariucci, they retorted, so poisoned the process that only a fool would have interviewed. The Rooney Rule, they insisted, was instituted precisely to prevent what Millen had done.

The debate raged in sports newsrooms across the nation all day, and that evening it took center stage in the sports world. ESPN, the undisputed sports media king, led *Sports Center*, its most popular news program, with the Detroit Lions hiring controversy. As the story spread, it seemed everyone with even a minimal interest in the NFL had an opinion as to the propriety of Millen's search. Ultimately, though, only one person's opinion really mattered, and despite the League-wide furor, Commissioner Tagliabue, whose task it would be to decide whether the Lions' violation merited a penalty, remained mum. Months earlier it had appeared that Tagliabue would be a Rooney Rule ally, if not a Rooney Rule champion. He had created the owners' and executives' committees to address the lack of diversity in the League's coaching ranks, and once the committees were constituted, he pressed owners for their support in expanding equal opportunity initiatives. Throughout the hiring season, however, he withheld comment on the rule's application, and although Mehri and Cochran publicly called for the League's involvement during the Jones-Parcells courtship, he said nothing. At his annual "state of the NFL" news conference, held on January 24, however, he had said plenty, and none of it seemed good for the Rooney Rule.

Confronted with a question about Mehri and Cochran's criticism of the Cowboys' and Jaguars' hiring processes, Tagliabue had bristled. He first took a shot at the two attorneys, explaining he had "respect for them as individuals" but questioning their usefulness to the NFL's equal opportunity efforts and ultimately describing their contributions as "mixed at best." He then turned to the substance of their complaints and expressed his frustration with their attacks on his League. "I don't understand what principle is supposed to underlie the criticism of the hiring of Bill Parcells and Jack Del Rio," Tagliabue railed. "The principle of fair employment really centers on the idea that employers should not hire unqualified or less-qualified people and pass over members of minority groups of one type or another who are more qualified or fully qualified. I don't see how that policy has been breached. I don't see what principle they are arguing for. Bill Parcells is a world-class coach. How can you criticize that?"

The comments flummoxed Mehri and Cochran. Tagliabue knew as well as anyone that the Rooney Rule was about process and that the point of demanding an inclusive process was to allow coaches of color who otherwise might be overlooked—and who, in fact, historically had been overlooked—a chance to argue their preparedness. Bill Parcells' status as a "world-class coach" was irrelevant. His status as the only coach considered for the job was what mattered.

Mehri and Cochran were loath to antagonize Tagliabue, with whom they believed they had forged a solid working relationship, but they fumed at what they saw to be transparent misdirection, and they counterattacked. Publicly accusing Tagliabue of being disingenuous and of undermining the very process he had helped create, Mehri characterized the commissioner's comments as blatantly signaling to the Lions the League's indifference to Rooney Rule enforcement.

The war of words ended there, with one volley in each direction. Pessimistic about Tagliabue's response to the Mariucci hire, however, Mehri and Cochran steeled themselves for action. If Tagliabue would not enforce the Rooney Rule in the Lions' case, it was hard to believe he would ever enforce it, and if he would never enforce it, then Mehri and Cochran had two choices: capitulate or fight. Mariucci's hire convinced them that blindly hoping teams would follow the rule with no threat of League enforcement was no longer an option. Yet they had come too far to capitulate. So with somber resignation they prepared emotionally for a legal battle they had hoped to avoid from the outset, one they were not sure they could win.

One aspect of Tagliabue's February 4 silence, however, suggested that the battle might not be necessary. Although Tagliabue proffered no opinion on the Mariucci matter and League spokesperson Greg Aiello was similarly muted, Aiello did indicate willingness to defer comment to Dan Rooney. In October, when Tagliabue appointed Rooney as diversity committee chairman, Wooten had told Mehri and Cochran that victory was in sight. Wooten's pronouncement seemed premature at the time, but Wooten had been envisioning a situation like the one that had now come to pass, a situation in which the diversity committee chairman would be called upon, in a moment of controversy, to set the League's tone and steer its response.

Rooney's reaction to the Lions' hiring rewarded Wooten's confidence. "The Lions' selection process," Rooney explained in a brief prepared statement, "fell short of what our committee recommends for all clubs as agreed in December. I will discuss this with the committee and the Lions to see what occurred and where to proceed in the future."

Although Rooney's comments were measured and noncommittal, they guaranteed that the League would not entirely ignore the Lions' conduct. Reporters pried, anxious for a hint of how the League would ultimately respond, but Rooney withheld further public comment. Privately, however, he seethed. He had worked hard to secure the owners' unanimous support, and as one among them, he himself was a party to the agreement. The Lions, Rooney felt, had been unfaithful to that agreement, and although he was famously slow to anger, he was deeply displeased. Whenever the League's top decision makers convened with Tagliabue to determine how to, as Rooney put it, "proceed in the future," there would be at least one person at the table intent on ensuring that no team repeated what the Lions had done.

Whether others at the table would share Rooney's perspective was not clear. With every passing day, however, it seemed more likely, as certified clout began lining up behind Mehri, Cochran, Wooten, and Winslow's call to punish the Lions.

First there was Gene Upshaw, who was among the most powerful people involved in professional football. As a Hall of Fame offensive guard with the Oakland Raiders from 1967 to 1981, Upshaw was the standard-bearer among linemen of his day and was undeniably one of the toughest and most respected players in the League at any position. His power, however, accrued after retirement: in 1983 he assumed the executive directorship of the NFL Players Association, then a relatively weak organization that served as the union for NFL players. Twenty years later, Upshaw remained executive director, but the union had changed drastically. Over the course of that time Upshaw had helped mold the NFLPA into a juggernaut that commanded the League's attention, and along the way he had established himself as a power broker. During Upshaw's tenure, players' salaries skyrocketed (as did his), and while many retired players questioned both the credit he deserved for the union's development and his seeming apathy toward the plight of those who had played in the League before the salary increases, Upshaw remained the union's undisputed leader and held sway over the League's most vital resource, its players.

So when Upshaw publicly attacked the Lions' hiring approach the day after Millen's press conference, asserting that the Lions treated "the agreed-upon minority hiring process almost as if it were a nuisance to their hiring of Steve Mariucci" and that "the minority candidates were never given a fair chance to interview," it meant something. While Upshaw was not speaking for the players, his influence among them gave his perspective substantial weight, and while there was no way to determine if his comments would prove persuasive to the NFL brass, they could not have gone unnoticed.

Upshaw, however, was just the beginning. What to this point had been essentially a sports story sprouted after the Lions' hiring into a bona fide national civil rights issue, and within days Jesse Jackson had entered the Rooney Rule fray, assailing the Lions' process and demanding that the NFL harshly penalize the team. Jackson brought with him both the gravitas and the disrepute he had accumulated during his decades of public life. Possessed of both "a magnificence of spirit and an appalling crassness," Jackson had inspired and infuriated throughout his career. On one hand, Jackson was the fearless civil rights advocate and powerful orator who founded the progressive Rainbow/PUSH Coalition and who won several Democratic primary contests during two impressive runs for the United States presidency. On the other, he was the man who had disgusted Martin Luther King Jr.'s widow, Coretta Scott King, in the aftermath of her husband's violent death by wearing a shirt stained with the civil rights leader's blood and parading it about for what appeared to be personal gain.

Love him or hate him, Jackson's concern about equality in sport was real, although the root of his passion on the issue was as cloudy and conflicted as the man himself. Jackson had been an undisputedly outstanding high school quarterback and talented all-around athlete, and after his high school career he received both a contract offer to play professional baseball and a football scholarship to the University of Illinois. He chose Illinois, and upon arriving in Champaign-Urbana in 1959 he showed early quarterbacking promise, once leading the freshman team to an intrasquad victory over the varsity. Soon, however, he was ordered to play halfback rather than quarterback and was then moved to the offensive line. The position switch demoralized Jackson, and he later attributed it to race, insisting his coaches told him "blacks could not be quarterbacks" at Illinois.

Such a rule would have been typical at the time. The NFL featured no African American quarterbacks, and aside from those playing at historically black colleges and universities, the collegiate ranks featured precious few. Jackson's explanation for his derailed quarterbacking ambitions during his freshman year at Illinois, therefore, made perfect sense—except that the facts seemed to refute it: Mel Meyers, the Illini's starting quarterback that year, was African American.

Whatever his genuine reasons, Jackson left the Illinois football team and ultimately transferred to North Carolina A&T, where he played quarterback and where he became increasingly interested in the burgeoning civil rights movement. Jackson's activist career would take off from there, but he never relinquished his love for football and over the years made it a point to decry racial inequity in the game. Indeed, in 2000, he had made headlines when he lamented the dearth of African American head coaches in the NFL, describing the League's hiring process as "a culture driven by white supremacists." Jackson had been relatively quiet on the issue since Mehri and Cochran launched their movement, but if the NFL failed to take the Lions to task, Rainbow/PUSH picket signs at 280 Park Avenue seemed a possibility.

Most striking of all, however, was that the people of Detroit, or at least their elected representatives, had turned against their hometown team. On February 12, seven days after Upshaw condemned the Lions and five days after Jackson did the same, the Detroit City Council passed a resolution expressing "disappointment in the Detroit Lions general manager and the Ford family" for ignoring the Rooney Rule mandate. The vote was unanimous and the rebuke passionate. Speaking for the council and to the spirit behind the vote, Councilman Alonzo Bates, who led the charge, explained, "I love sports. I'm a member of the Super Bowl 2005 host committee. But

I'm also an activist. I graduated from Alabama State in 1964. I marched and demonstrated for civil rights. It's ridiculous we're still dealing with this kind of issue in professional football."

Neither Upshaw, Jackson, Bates, nor the other city council members would be present when NFL officials gathered to discuss the Lions' hiring process, but their perspectives would be there, if only in the officials' collective subconscious. So too would be vestiges of the countless conversations League officials had had with Mehri and Cochran on the issue as well as the legal threat the two lawyers had first made months earlier. Theirs, however, was not the only Rooney Rule–related legal threat facing the NFL. The Lions organization was furious with what it deemed unfair public attacks, and Ford, who had been a stalwart NFL supporter throughout his thirty-nine years as the Lions' owner, was reportedly willing to turn to the courts if the League imposed any penalty he deemed to be unfair.

Rocks and hard places were everywhere, but Tagliabue and his lieutenants would not be meeting officially with Lions executives about the Mariucci hiring until early March and likely would not issue a determination until well after that meeting, so they had time to grapple with the various considerations that might inform their decision.

On February 21, however, before League officials were able to fully engage the issue of Rooney Rule enforcement, the NFL's landscape unexpectedly shifted in a manner that would heavily impact the League's future and, potentially, its leaders' deliberations.

8

BIRTH OF AN ALLIANCE

WHAT MEHRI AND COCHRAN HAD ACCOMPLISHED in just five months far exceeded their wildest expectations. They had built strong working relationships with Wooten and Winslow and, through them, with other powerful and respected African American figures in the professional football community. Together with those allies, they had convinced the NFL to study itself and, ultimately, to reform. They had proposed the reformatory mechanism, the Rooney Rule, that the League eventually adopted. And through their work, opportunity was expanding for the League's coaches of color. Sure, the Cowboys' and Lions' interview processes were disappointing, but Mehri and Cochran hoped that in the coming months Commissioner Tagliabue would equip the Rooney Rule with an enforcement mechanism, and they were confident that if he did, such noncompliant interview processes would soon be few and far between.

One concern other than uncertainty regarding the commissioner's next move tempered their joy. As dedicated as Mehri and Cochran were to creating equal opportunity for coaches of color in the NFL, they knew the fight was not truly theirs. For months they had been working on behalf of the NFL coaches whose fight it was, but they had met only a few. Wooten and Winslow had certainly served to connect Mehri and Cochran to those for whom they were advocating, but they were still fundamentally outsiders. If their efforts were to blossom into a self-sustaining movement for equality, the primary stakeholders, the coaches themselves, would have to engage the battle. Mehri and Cochran worried that the coaches would not do so, that they would be afraid to publicly represent or even support the movement. It was the same concern that, months earlier, had convinced them that finding a plaintiff for what was then a prospective lawsuit against the NFL would be nearly impossible.

But the time had come to face that concern. A groundswell among coaches would send a powerful signal and, they believed, might well influence Commissioner Tagliabue to punish the Lions and strengthen the rule. Even if not, it would certainly invigorate the movement and increase pressure on the League. Mehri and Cochran resolved that they had to gather the coaches together and get them on board. Wooten agreed, and he knew there was only one place to do it: the NFL Scouting Combine.

The Combine is the one event on the NFL calendar during which all of the League's coaches are in one place at one time, and it therefore presented an ideal opportunity for Mehri and Cochran to meet and try to galvanize the individuals they were hoping to help. Wooten, Younger, and Gilliam had over the years used the occasion to engage fellow African Americans in the League on issues confronting them all. Previous meetings had never progressed much beyond venting sessions, but now that the Rooney Rule was in place and expert lawyers were on their side, Wooten believed, the 2003 Combine might be different.

To the uninitiated, the Combine is a startling spectacle. Held in Indianapolis every February, after the collegiate football season but before the NFL draft, it features the nation's top collegiate football players in a dizzying week-long exhibition of speed, strength, and football skill. NFL teams' coaches and front office executives observe the workouts, assess the players, and use the information they obtain to determine whom to select in the draft. For many players, the Combine is their best chance to sufficiently impress a team to land a spot in an NFL training camp. For others, a good Combine showing means a higher draft slot and, along with it, higher remuneration once in the League.

Notably, the players do not actually play football games at the Combine. Instead, they engage in various drills and exercises designed to test every aspect of a prospect's physical being. They run, jump, stretch, press weights, and endure assorted pokes and prods as team officials scan their bodies for flaws. Although highly organized, it is at base a meat market, and because the athletes are primarily African American and the officials scrutinizing every muscle twitch are primarily white, the Combine, when historically contextualized, presents a disconcerting image. Indeed, some commentators have asserted that, minus the pomp and pageantry, the annual ritual harks back to the slave block. Others, citing the seven- and eight-figure salaries for which the athletes are auditioning, dismiss such comparison as inapt. Neither Mehri nor Cochran had ever ventured into this debate, but even putting slavery allusions to the side, the Combine's power dynamics were obvious. For the most part, whites were the brains and African Americans were the brawn, making the Combine a concrete, real-time manifestation of their concern with the NFL. It was the perfect place to organize for change.

What seemed like a great idea in the planning, however, seemed less so on February 20, the meeting's eve. Things were not materializing as Mehri had hoped. Weeks earlier, Mehri's assistant, Jaki Lee, had sent invitations to African American coaches, front office personnel, and scouts throughout the League. Few responded, and Mehri feared an embarrassingly low turnout. Worse than that, whoever did show would surely be disappointed not to see Cochran. The invitation promised Cochran's presence, and Cochran had planned to be there, but as often happened, late-breaking developments in Cochran's schedule made his presence impossible.

As talented a lawyer as Mehri was, he suffered no delusions about his stature vis-à-vis Cochran's. Virtually everybody in the nation, whether or not affiliated with the legal community, knew of Cochran. Virtually nobody outside of the legal community knew of Mehri. Some of the meeting's attendees might be coming just to meet Cochran, and Mehri was simply no substitute. Moreover, Mehri lacked Cochran's rhetorical flourish. He had seen Cochran stir a room and galvanize people with his words, and Mehri couldn't do it, at least not to the same extent. Mehri anticipated that most people who showed up would be reluctant to get involved in the equal opportunity effort and would need convincing, and he was not sure he could prompt them into action as Cochran certainly would have been able to do. Put plainly, he was nervous that he, and the meeting, would fail.

Wooten, on the other hand, never seemed to get nervous, and as he and Mehri sat down for dinner that evening he held true to form. Perhaps at some point in the old warrior's life he had gotten nervous, but if so, he'd seemingly lost the ability. Like Mehri, Wooten was disappointed Cochran would be absent, and although Wooten knew virtually all the invitees and regularly communicated with many of them, he was no more certain than Mehri as to how many people would show up. Still, even without Cochran or much of a crowd, Wooten believed the meeting could be successful. The key would be Mehri connecting with the attendees, and Mehri would not have to orate like Cochran to do it. Of course, Mehri couldn't speak the way he would in a courtroom, either—there would be no judges or lawyers in the room, no legal precedents or statutes to cite. If ever a speaker faced a situation in which he had to adjust to his audience, this was it.

"Cyrus, these guys are football guys," Wooten explained between bites of standard hotel fare. "You have to talk to them like football guys."

There was no insult in Wooten's words. In a battle of wits, he would have gladly pitted his football guys against all comers. He knew, however, how they thought and how they learned. A theoretical exposition would be largely ineffective. To gain traction, Mehri had to package his ideas as crisp, concise nuggets and deliver them one after another in quick succession. And it would be best to accompany his points graphically, so a chalkboard or dry erase board would help. In essence, Wooten was calling for something analogous to the X's and O's of football playmaking. He wanted Mehri to present the attendees with a game plan and explain to them their roles in it.

Mehri had never delivered a presentation in quite the way Wooten was requesting, but the following day's meeting was at four o'clock in the afternoon, giving him plenty of time to prepare. By the appointed hour, Mehri was ready. He had not tracked down a chalkboard or dry erase board, but at the front of the meeting room he had set up a large newsprint pad on an easel. He figured it would suffice.

Slowly invitees began making their way into the room, and before long they numbered roughly a dozen. Mehri was relieved. They had double digits, enough for a productive meeting. But the number kept growing, and Mehri realized they hadn't requested enough chairs from the hotel—some people staked out positions against the wall, while others sat on the floor. The room had grown so crowded that when Wooten and Winslow arrived, they had difficulty winding their way through the bodies to join Mehri near the easel. By the time the last few invitees trickled in, the group numbered well over one hundred. It felt as though every African American coach, scout, and front office official in the NFL was there.

Whoever was closest to the door pulled it shut, and Wooten called the meeting to order, welcoming all in attendance and emphasizing the importance of the moment. Beyond that, Wooten did not say much. Often under such circumstances he would wax eloquent about historical context. On this occasion, he seemed anxious to move the meeting along, hoping the individuals in the room would embrace the opportunity to formally organize.

Winslow spoke next, briefly airing frustrations he knew all in the room shared and then matter-of-factly announcing: "Right now, all of your names are Paul." After a pause, he explained the non sequitur, telling them that he had just finished reading a biography of A. Philip Randolph, the civil rights activist and organizer who in 1937 unionized the African American railroad porters working for the Pullman Company. George Pullman founded the company in 1862, and by the mid-1920s it was the nation's largest employer of African American labor. The porters, numbering more than twenty thousand at their peak, were nameless, faceless, cogs in the Pullman machine before Randolph organized them; so nameless and faceless, in fact, that the train passengers they served addressed each and every one of them simply as "George" after George Pullman.

Winslow asserted that while certainly better situated than the porters had been eighty years earlier, most of the men in the room were, in the League's owners' view, similarly nameless and faceless.

"The people who run this league don't know you," Winslow charged, "so for all practical purposes, they may as well refer to you as Paul, à la Paul Tagliabue.

"You can't get the job," he continued, "if they don't know who you are, and they won't know who you are until you organize."

With the group still contemplating the weight of Winslow's analogy, Mehri took the floor. He spoke briefly about the report, the fledging Rooney Rule, and the equal opportunity gains being made in the NFL, but he was conscious not to meander. He had been speaking for less than a minute when he made his principal point: "To win this fight, you're going to have to form an affinity group to represent your interests." Mehri turned, wrote "Affinity Group" at the top of his newsprint pad, and then whipped back around to face his audience. "You are stronger together than you are individually. An affinity group allows you to stand together."

In settling class-action racial discrimination cases, Mehri had always insisted that companies provide resources for their employees to form affinity groups so the employees could collectively challenge the company from within if discrimination resurfaced in the future. Almost without exception, the affinity groups greatly empowered the employees, increased their clout within the company, and contributed to increased organizational equal opportunity. Mehri knew if the people in the room formed an affinity group, the NFL would have to recognize it and respect its power.

The affinity group would have three missions. The first, he explained, writing a bullet point on the newsprint, would be advocacy. True change required them to advocate for themselves. Their collective voice was more powerful than either his or Cochran's. They had to be the ones to hammer home the Rooney Rule's virtues if they expected Commissioner Tagliabue to give it teeth. And they had to be the watchdogs to ensure that teams complied. Otherwise, Mehri warned, the movement's momentum would quickly fizzle.

Both Mehri's confidence and his exuberance were now increasing. "The group's second mission," he said while scribbling a second bullet point, "would be developing, cultivating, and mentoring within the group, so that the base of candidates gets stronger and stronger." For decades, NFL decision makers had resisted calls for coaching and front office diversity with claims that few qualified candidates of color existed. Mehri and Cochran had attacked that premise with their report, and the pool of talent in the room flatly invalidated it. Still, through teaching, assisting, and uplifting each other, they could further develop that talent pool and forever silence those questioning their preparedness.

Finally, with one last turn to the newsprint, Mehri concluded that the affinity group would never succeed without communication. Neither advocacy nor mentoring would be effective without it. After the Combine, those in the room would disperse across the country, to major cities such as New York as well as smaller, remote towns such as Green Bay, Wisconsin. It was crucial that they establish an efficient means of communication and that they utilize it to keep everyone informed about both potential career opportunities and common concerns.

That was it. Mehri had said all he had to say. He wasn't sure he had done what Wooten wanted. Rather than presenting a game plan, it seemed he had set out a vision. Before he could fully scrutinize his presentation, however, the gathering began to buzz. An anxious energy filled the room as numerous whispered conversations erupted among the attendees.

The meeting's ultimate outcome was as yet untold, but already there was victory in it. For the first time, the League's off-field African Americans were, as a group, earnestly contemplating organizing. In four decades of NFL affiliation, Wooten had never seen anything like it.

Eventually the whispered conversations gave way to a full-blown discussion through which coursed, in roughly equal parts, excitement and fear. These were well-paid employees in one of the nation's most glamorous industries, but they could just as easily have been low-wage factory workers at an anonymous corporation somewhere in the American heartland. They relished the possibility of forming a united front and expanding their opportunities, but they feared reprisals.

Early in the discussion it seemed fear would trump everything else and that open conversation would be the only victory to emerge from the meeting. For many in the room, the potential downside just seemed too great, and after several attendees expressed their concerns in somewhat guarded language, one among them turned to Mehri and succinctly articulated what appeared the prevailing view.

"You don't understand how the owners are. Heads are going to roll. They're going to come down on this and people will lose jobs."

There was little Mehri could say. He would do his best to guard them against unlawful termination, but he knew that when courts adjudicated employment discrimination and retaliation actions they often deferred to defendants' subjective assessments of their employees, particularly in the sports context. If the owners did seek to penalize the people in the room, Mehri could not guarantee he would be able to protect them. There was no way to completely avoid risk, and if the coaches, scouts, and executives were unwilling to accept that, as the tenor of the comments suggested, they would never become an affinity group. Mehri had been successful in sparking debate, but at that stage in the meeting his success did not seem likely to extend beyond that.

Then Terry Robiskie stood up.

Robiskie was not the most decorated man in the room, but he had worked as an assistant coach in the League for twenty years. He had been denied opportunities for which he felt perfectly suited and had seen less prepared white coaches promoted past him on more occasions than he cared to recount. He'd had enough.

"If heads are going to roll, let it be my head," he announced.

Robiskie was not bombastic in his statement, but he was passionate, and he was obviously not posturing. If organizing for increased opportunity cost him his job, he was willing to accept the loss.

Robiskie's words deeply impacted the meeting's tone. They reframed the entire discussion around the idea of courage. The men in the room could either stand up, at some risk, against discrimination they had all witnessed, or sit back and let it continue. Each man had choices to make, and one by one the individuals in the room made them. Comments similar to Robiskie's, if less pointed and impassioned, began cascading.

Before long, Tony Dungy took the floor. Dungy commanded enormous respect among those in attendance, and as the longest-tenured of the League's three African American head coaches, he had given some of the attendees their first jobs in the NFL. "If we're all in it together," Dungy calmly insisted, "we can make this work."

Just over a year earlier, Dungy had inspired Mehri with his grace in the face of what was, in Mehri's view, an indubitably discriminatory dismissal. Now, it seemed, Mehri had inspired Dungy, and with Dungy on board, the matter was essentially closed. If anybody in the room still opposed organizing, he did so silently.

Wooten struggled to control his emotions. For years he and a handful of allies had worked in the shadows, trying, with limited success, to expand opportunities for people of color in the NFL. They had few resources, no public presence, and little leverage with the League. He now stood in a room with well over one hundred individuals who were prepared to band together in pressing the NFL for equal opportunity and a lawyer who had proven committed to their cause.

Winslow too was moved. He was blessed to have had many big moments in his life, and this ranked among the biggest. Perhaps, he thought as he watched the meeting unfold, this group would help create opportunities such as those he anticipated having when he retired from the game. After all, he had children, one of whom, also named Kellen, was a star tight end at the University of Miami. If the younger Kellen eventually made it to the NFL, maybe upon retirement he would have greater opportunities than his father ever had to become a power broker in the League.

Mehri simply soaked it all in. Emotion did not overcome him as it did Wooten and Winslow. It couldn't. He had not fought the fights they had. He did, however, feel tremendous professional satisfaction. His efforts had helped birth an organization, and gazing out across the room, he sensed its potential power. He was already thinking about next steps, among them what name might suit the group. Through studying football's history, Mehri had learned about Fritz Pollard, the outstanding running back who earned All-American honors at Brown University early in the twentieth century while leading Brown to its first and only Rose Bowl appearance. Mehri also learned that upon leaving Brown, Pollard went on to play, and then serve as a player/coach, in the NFL's predecessor, the American Professional Football Association.

Pollard's story, Mehri discovered, was amazing. As one of the APFA's few African American players and its only African American head coach, every game Pollard played was reflective of the broader societal battle being waged outside of the stadium. He was, as much as a person can be while playing a game, under siege, enduring such consistent brutality after being tackled that, to protect against a career-ending injury or worse, he developed a mechanism of punishing those who sought to punish him. Upon hitting the ground after a tackle, Pollard rolled onto his back, raised his feet in the air, and waved them as if riding a bicycle while simultaneously propelling himself to an upright position. Any opponent seeking to cheap-shot Pollard as he was getting up ran the risk of being kicked.

Unfortunately, Pollard's career ended prematurely when the League segregated, and by 1989, when the League next featured an African American head coach, Pollard had passed away and had largely receded into history's footnotes.

This was the perfect opportunity, Mehri thought, to resurrect Pollard's name and accomplishments. Naming the organization in Pollard's memory would ground it historically and honor the individual who had preceded everyone in the room. Mehri hoped the others in the room would support his idea, and when they later discussed it, they overwhelmingly did. Going forward, they agreed, they would be the Fritz Pollard Alliance (FPA), with Winslow as their executive director and Wooten as their chairman.

Suddenly Mehri and Cochran had a client, and the NFL faced a new dynamic. The external threat the lawyers presented, through the media if not through the courts, was now coupled with internal pressure. Together, the lawyers and the FPA's members lobbied for a stronger Rooney Rule, on one occasion meeting with NFL officials at the NFL's offices to press their case, but for months the League made no public comment about Millen's search for a head coach.

To those hoping for a stiff penalty, the League's silence may have suggested a deprioritization of the Rooney Rule and its enforcement. In fact, it reflected neither. On the contrary, it reflected the enormousness of the issue. Tagliabue was not a man who reacted off the cuff. Rather, he valued patience. Indeed, among his reasons for ultimately supporting the Rooney Rule was his view that it would slow the coaching carousel and promote more careful deliberation among the League's clubs. Now, faced with the most important decision in the fledgling rule's short existence, he would not be rushed—not by Jesse Jackson, the Detroit City Council, or any other interested party. In fact, the increasingly intense public debate decreased any inclination Tagliabue might have had to render a quick decision. "The more outside commentary there was," Jeff Pash later explained of the prevailing sense at 280 Park Avenue, "the more we felt we're going to wait until temperatures come down a bit and until everyone's blood pressure gets a little lower, and then we'll address what really happened and respond to it in an appropriate and proportionate way."

Rather than rushing to judgment, Tagliabue and his top advisors launched an investigation, scrutinizing the events surrounding the Lions' hire and interviewing involved parties. They spoke on multiple occasions with Lions personnel, including Millen and Ford, and they also spoke with Tim Lewis, who had declined Millen's interview offer, all with an eye toward deducing precisely how the Lions' process had transpired.

After investigating the matter, Tagliabue convened the owners' and executives' committees to process the gathered information and discuss whether Millen had, in fact, preordained the search's outcome and therefore deserved blame for violating the Rooney Rule. In the end, though, the decision was Tagliabue's to make, and in making it, he had to resolve one ultimate question: would penalizing the Lions be in the best interests of the National Football League?

In 1921, little more than a year after members of Major League Baseball's Chicago White Sox infamously accepted money in exchange for losing the 1919 World Series, MLB owners hired Judge Kennesaw Mountain Landis as league commissioner and charged him with doing whatever was necessary to protect the "best interests" of baseball. During the following years and decades, as new professional leagues formed and as team owners appointed commissioners, they granted their hires the same quantum of power. The NFL was no exception.

Ultimately, Tagliabue's investigation revealed that Millen had so clearly committed to hiring Mariucci that the coaches of color who refused the interview with the Lions could not be faulted. The Lions' Rooney Rule violation, therefore, constituted "conduct detrimental" to the League and necessitated a penalty. But determining the scope of the penalty created a secondary problem. If the penalty was too harsh, the rule could lose credibility and, in turn, ownership support. The owners had voted the rule in, and if they deemed the penalty too severe, they could, with a three-quarters vote, abandon the rule altogether. In fact, they could go further and abandon Tagliabue. He served at their pleasure. They did not serve at his. Without ownership support he could not effectively function as league commissioner. On the other hand, an insufficiently meaningful penalty would encourage other clubs to disregard the nascent rule, thereby gutting it. Tagliabue's task was to thread the needle.

On July 25, 2003, almost six months after the Lions hired Mariucci, Tagliabue delivered his decision, assessing Millen a $200,000 fine for failing to discharge his duties under the Rooney Rule. The League rarely issued executives such substantial fines and generally did so only for salary cap violations and other major transgressions. The penalty thus established the Rooney Rule among the League's most sacred mandates. The commissioner did not stop with the penalty, however, issuing a warning as well. The next Rooney Rule violation, he announced, would trigger a $500,000 fine.

The newly constituted FPA was euphoric. "On behalf of FPA's members," executive director Kellen Winslow announced through an immediate press release, "I am happy to applaud the league for making the Rooney Rule enforceable, which is a major step in leveling the playing field in the NFL. We are pleased that the rule now has teeth and hope today's announcement sends a strong message to owners to embrace inclusive hiring practices going forward."

Ford was as displeased as Winslow was pleased. "I think it's a shame and totally unwarranted," Ford fumed, explaining that when Tagliabue called to detail the decision, he became increasingly angry with the commissioner, eventually hanging up on him. "I've lost a lot of respect for the Commissioner because of the way he's handled this."

Ultimately, as much as Ford and the Lions' other officials complained, they did not seek legal redress, and Ford did not rescind his agreement to the rule, choosing to formally "disagree" with Tagliabue's decision but going no further. Among owners, Ford was not alone in disagreement, but like Ford, the others honored the handshake commitment they had made seven months earlier. The center held.

Tagliabue had done his job. He had enforced the rule without destroying it. In fact, in a separate proclamation, he strengthened it, clarifying that compliance required that teams' top-level administrators, rather than their underlings, conduct the Rooney Rule interviews and that they do so in person.

Still, there was nothing Tagliabue could do to convince skeptics that the rule's beneficiaries were deserving of the mandated interviews. Indeed, in the penalty's wake, an expanding cadre of commentators assailed the rule as unfairly advantaging head coaching candidates of color. At the time, Marvin Lewis was the only head coach of color to have been hired since the rule's December 21 enactment, and fairly or not, as the NFL's 2003 season began, Rooney Rule supporters and detractors alike associated Lewis with the League's new equal opportunity efforts. A successful season would validate the rule. Failure would undermine it. All eyes were on the Bengals.

9

A SEASON OF DREAMS

NFL GAMES ARE WON during the off-season. Although the League's season and postseason generally run from September through early February, the spring and summer make champions. Crucial to a strong spring is the League's annual draft, during which teams have the opportunity to upgrade their rosters with fresh collegiate talent. In 2003 the Bengals, by virtue of their last-place finish among the League's thirty-two teams the previous year, possessed the draft's first pick.

Unfortunately, by most accounts, the draft pool did not contain a single franchise player. Several excellent players, such as quarterbacks Carson Palmer and Byron Leftwich, wide receiver Charles Rogers, and cornerback Terence Newman, were available, but talent evaluators generally agreed none of them would be a surefire NFL star. Rather than using the first pick, the Bengals had the option of trading it in exchange for a lower pick and other considerations, but because other teams were similarly uninspired by the top draft entrants, the Bengals received little interest. "The phone is not exactly ringing off the hook," Lewis said at the time. "If we go to [other teams], we won't get a very good deal."

So it was that Lewis began his tenure with the gift of the draft's top pick, but in a down year for the draft. It was simple bad luck, and nothing Lewis could control. Everything he could control, however, he did. Even before the draft, he started revamping the organization's culture, signaling in a variety of ways that a new day had dawned for the Bengals. He began by convincing everyone who would listen that the Bengals were not cursed, that there was, as he put it, "no old ship's pirate or captain who knows we're on his burial site." He then turned to a bevy of simple, concrete initiatives.

For instance, Lewis upgraded the weight room to place it on par with other NFL teams' strengthening facilities and arranged for lunch to be served at the Bengals' complex during the off-season, something the team had never before done. His efforts yielded immediate dividends, as his players foresaw the possibility of their team progressing beyond doormat status. In previous years, scarcely ten players would turn up for the first day of the team's off-season conditioning program. The 2003 program's first day attracted more than forty. In addition, Lewis ensured first-class treatment for free agents visiting Cincinnati, and the club ultimately made several key free agent acquisitions.

No off-season development was more symbolic than the gesture the team made toward its starting quarterback, Jon Kitna. Under Kitna's contract, being on the field for 80 percent of the team's plays in 2002 entitled him to a $1.625 million bonus. Kitna missed the threshold by six plays, but breaking away from its miserly organizational reputation, the Bengals paid the bonus anyway. Lewis certainly did not control the Bengals' purse strings, but it was hard to imagine that he didn't influence the decision.

By April, the Bengals already appeared to be a new team. "The new coach," one journalist noted, "brought the organization from the 19th century to the 21st century in less than three months."

But Lewis was not nearly done. As summer approached, dissatisfied with the Bengals' training camp facilities in Georgetown,

Kentucky, he asked for, and received, an additional large meeting room as well as additional practice space. Once at camp, he learned every individual's name—from the cooks to the secretaries—establishing by example that everyone involved in the Bengals' effort to improve was important. When it came to his players, he approached them in innovative ways and with innovative ideas, regularly utilizing multimedia presentations to drive home his points. He also attended to often underemphasized aspects of professional athletes' lives, organizing, for instance, a seminar in which a nutritionist addressed best dietary practices and another in which a Cincinnati police representative conversed with players about how best to approach disagreements with law enforcement officers.

On the field, improvement was steady. With that first pick in the draft, the Bengals ultimately settled on Palmer, the Heisman Trophy–winning quarterback from the University of Southern California, and although Kitna would be the starting quarterback come fall, Palmer was developing nicely and looked to be the quarterback of the future. The rest of the squad was progressing as well, as Lewis pushed his players through workout after intensely challenging workout, quickly assessing their talent, work ethic, and commitment to his program and dismissing those who consistently made mental mistakes or displayed lackadaisical attitudes. As summer wound down, the largely revamped Bengals throbbed with optimism, and on August 10 they had the opportunity to reveal their new selves in their preseason opening game against the New York Jets.

Generally, preseason games are not terribly meaningful or indicative of an NFL team's strength. They don't factor into the team's official record, and because coaches use them to evaluate as many players as possible, they usually involve frequent, rhythm-inhibiting substitutions. But this was no ordinary preseason game. There was, as *New York Times* journalist Gerald Eskenazi described, a "romantic notion" in it. It was the resurrected Bengals' first game, a chance to display their newly inculcated spirit and pride. And it was "the Heisman Trophy winner and overall No. 1 draft pick, in his first pro game, playing for a rookie head coach who knows he has to change the culture of a losing team." Ultimately, however, it was a disaster, and by game's end the romance had long faded. The Bengals made the sorts of mistakes bad teams make. They bungled an extra-point attempt as well as a field goal attempt, and they turned the ball over an unacceptable four times, twice in the game's final two minutes via Carson Palmer interceptions, both of which Jets defenders returned for touchdowns.

As displeased as Lewis was with his team's performance, he was, in his own words, excited. He knew his team would make mistakes, and now, with the mistakes on tape, he was anxious to launch his analysis and improve upon them.

Lewis would have his chance the following week when the Bengals hosted the Detroit Lions in their second preseason game. At the previous season's conclusion, the Bengals and Lions held the League's two worst records, winning a combined five out of thirty-two games, and the contest between the cellar dwellers promised to be quite possibly the least compelling NFL game played that year. For Lewis and the Bengals, though, it mattered mightily. They yearned to cleanse themselves of the Jets debacle, and a win would certainly help. In addition, the game represented the Bengals' home debut as a newly reconstituted team. Lewis had spent the off-season making public appearances in and around Cincinnati in hopes of cultivating goodwill and reviving the city's interest in its football team. The time had come to present Cincinnati with a product it could support and grow to love.

When the Bengals took the field to meet the Lions, the stands in Paul Brown Stadium were sparsely filled. The team sold fewer tickets than it had for any preseason game since the stadium opened three years earlier, evidence that Bengals fans were on the whole unconvinced the team would be worth watching. Those who did attend witnessed a rarity: the Bengals won, and they did so in style. Palmer played beautifully, replacing Kitna in the second half and completing all seven of his passes while leading the Bengals on two impressive touchdown drives and sparking a standing ovation from the faithful. Granted, the Lions were far from a defensive powerhouse and Palmer did his work against their second-string players, but

Palmer and the rest of the team were showing progress. "We did what we said we wanted, which was to improve from last week," Lewis said after the game. "We're getting better."

The following week the Tennessee Titans traveled to Cincinnati for a game the Bengals hoped would build on the previous week's success. The NFL preseason's third game is generally its most revealing, as teams, having dedicated substantial portions of the two previous games to assessing backups, give their starters significant playing time before resting them in the fourth and final preseason game. Rather than shining against the Titans in their dress rehearsal for the regular season, however, the Bengals sputtered, looking hapless against Titans quarterback Steve McNair and repeatedly self-destructing on offense en route to an uninspired 23–15 loss.

A week later the Bengals headed to Indianapolis to face the Colts and again lost. With that defeat, the Bengals closed their preseason at 1–3, an inauspicious beginning. Still, there was a sense around the Cincinnati locker room that this losing Bengals squad was different from previous losing Bengals squads. Even in loss there was an arrogance of sorts, a sense that this team was above the losing tradition in which they were enmeshed. In short, the losers felt like winners, and it all emanated from Lewis. Even Chad Johnson, the Bengals' talented but notoriously enigmatic and often intractable wide receiver, was happy. "I'm loving it," Johnson proclaimed as the Bengals prepared for their first regular-season game under Lewis. "Coach Lewis has a swagger. He has a cocky sense to him. Everything is going in the right direction." Despite the 1–3 preseason and the poor performances that characterized most of it, the Bengals *knew*, because Lewis had convinced them, that they were growing into a good team.

On September 7, with that confidence, the Bengals opened their regular season at home against the Denver Broncos. Wearing redesigned all-black uniforms, the Bengals stormed onto the field to claim victory, and promptly got crushed 30–10. Before the Bengals scored their first touchdown, most of the sellout crowd had conceded defeat and left the stadium. On the surface, it seemed nothing had changed. "Eight months of preparation and 24 new players," wrote *Cincinnati*

Enquirer journalist Mark Curnutte, "produced a game that was eerily similar to the 34–6 opening-day loss a year ago."

In fact, everything had changed. It just hadn't yet become apparent.

Lewis urged patience. "We're here for the long haul," he insisted to the assembled press during the game's postmortem. "It's not a sprint. This is more like a marathon." Then, speaking more to the fans than the reporters, he added, "Hang with us, we'll be back."

On September 14, still confident, the Bengals traveled to Oakland and lost by three points to the reigning AFC champion Raiders. The Bengals played well, coming back from behind on multiple occasions before Raiders kicker Sebastian Janikowski drilled a thirty-nine-yard field goal to cement the victory. Cincinnati was obviously much improved, but none of the Bengals claimed moral victory because their coach had trained them not to. The loss, although valiant, was unsatisfactory. "Like Marvin says, moral victories are for losers," explained four-year Bengals veteran Oliver Gibson. "Expectations are a lot higher than they've been."

On September 21, back in Cincinnati and even more confident than the week before, the Bengals played the Pittsburgh Steelers. The Bengals made several critical mistakes and lost 17–10 in a game that was less competitive than the final score indicated. Shielding his players after their third straight loss, Lewis absorbed the blame. "Today, we got beat by a team that made more plays than we did. It's my job to find us a way to make plays to win this football game. We're not making plays in the critical situations that it takes to win the game, and that is my responsibility." Refusing to dwell on the defeat, Lewis looked forward and prepared for the Bengals' September 28 showdown in Cleveland with the Browns.

Before Paul Brown founded the Bengals, he coached the Browns for the franchise's first nineteen seasons, leaving only after Art Modell, who bought the team in 1961, forced him out. Brown detested Modell, and their feud became a Bengals-Browns feud. Decades later, the teams remained bitter rivals, making their September 28 meeting a huge game for both.

Objectively, there seemed little reason for the Bengals to maintain the confidence that had propelled them through the season's first three games. Although they had narrowly lost on the road to a strong Raiders team, they were nonetheless 0–3, and they had not led any of their games at any point. Furthermore, the playoffs, every team's season goal, were a near statistical impossibility, as just 4 of the 105 teams to begin a season 0–3 since 1978 had qualified for the postseason. Worse yet, their star running back, Corey Dillon, was nursing a pulled groin muscle, which had prevented him from playing during the second half against the Steelers and rendered him questionable for the Browns game.

Still, the Bengals entered the game with what had become their characteristic confidence. During those eight off-season months about which Mark Curnutte dismissively wrote after the Bengals' season-opening loss, Lewis had toiled to strengthen the Bengals' collective psyche, to convince them they were winners even though on paper they were not. He had prepared them to prevail when losing seemed the natural course, and he promised they eventually would win. Finally they did.

Although the Browns were favored, the Bengals worked hard and Lewis pushed all the right buttons. During the second quarter, for instance, with his team losing 14–7 and his defense playing sloppy, penalty-ridden football, Lewis, a defensive coordinator at heart, gathered his defensive unit on the sideline to both excoriate and instruct them. The Browns would not score again that quarter or for the balance of the game. And at halftime, before returning to the Bengals' locker room, Lewis approached the game officials and notified them of illegal finger movements the Browns quarterback was making at the line of scrimmage, which were drawing Bengals defenders offside. Attuned to the issue, officials called only one offside penalty against the Bengals in the second half and penalized the Browns four times for false starts.

Once the Bengals seized the lead with nine minutes and one second remaining in the third quarter, they never relinquished it, and when the game clock expired, they had logged their first victory. The

Bengals celebrated, of course, but as one reporter covering the game observed, they "didn't scream, dance or do anything stupid." Instead, they acted as if they had been there before, as if winning was routine, and soon it would become just that.

The following week, the Bengals traveled to Buffalo and played well but lost in overtime to the Bills. Thereafter, however, they began a magical run of the sort Lewis had envisioned all along, shocking opponents and eclipsing milestones.

In Cincinnati's next game, the Bengals beat the AFC North division-leading Baltimore Ravens 34–26, and in doing so unleashed their strongest offensive performance since 1999. A week later, they beat the NFC West division-leading Seattle Seahawks 27–24, establishing their first two-game win streak in two years. Long pejoratively dubbed the "Cincinnati Bungles" for their often endless parade of in-game mistakes, these Bengals were perfect with the ball against both the Ravens and the Seahawks, committing zero turnovers. It was, as *Cincinnati Enquirer* journalist Paul Daugherty gushed, "as if the 2003 Bengals recently arrived from another planet."

After a disappointing three-point loss to the Arizona Cardinals on November 2, the Bengals returned to winning, prevailing in consecutive games over the Houston Texans, the theretofore undefeated Kansas City Chiefs, the San Diego Chargers, and the Pittsburgh Steelers.

Twelve games into the season, the Bengals were an astounding 7–5 and tied for the division lead. The players, once pariahs in their own city, were suddenly heroes. Running back Brandon Bennett, one of the longest-serving Bengals, had spent his six years in Cincinnati risking harassment when venturing into public places, but suddenly the harassment vanished and everything in town was gratis: "You go out to eat, and people are buying you drinks, paying for your meal, letting you have it for free." His teammates experienced the same surreal attitudinal shift. Once-quiet walks through the airport gave way to harried, autograph-intensive sojourns. Cameo appearances at high school athletic contests became mob scenes. When the Bengals played at home, the entire city reveled and the sold-out Paul Brown

Stadium crowd's jubilation echoed through the downtown streets. And inside the stadium, the epicenter of the madness, hung a banner simply reading, "In Marvin We Trust."

Marvin Lewis had resurrected a franchise and invigorated a city, and every coach-of-the-year conversation throughout the League included his name. He had "walked into a sinkhole, and overnight there were tulips everywhere."

With four games remaining, the playoffs were a strong possibility. Pundits were certain the Bengals would beat the lowly 49ers in Cincinnati and similarly certain they would lose in St. Louis, where the Rams—dubbed "The Greatest Show on Turf" for the high-scoring offensive outbursts they routinely produced on their artificial-grass home field—had not lost in thirteen games. If so, to finish the season at 9–7 and position themselves for a potential playoff birth, the Bengals would have to beat either the Ravens or the Browns, both divisional rivals the Bengals had already defeated once that season. The 49ers and Rams games went as predicted, and the Bengals lost in Baltimore to the Ravens, leaving the Bengals one game to play at home against the Browns for a chance at the 2003 postseason as well as universal renown for perhaps the greatest organizational turnaround in NFL history.

On December 28, 2003, sixty-five thousand Bengals fans piled into Paul Brown Stadium desperately hoping for a victory and a celebration, but the Browns, and their running backs in particular, did not cooperate. They ran over, through, and around the Bengals defense, accumulating 264 yards on the day, more rushing yardage than the Bengals had allowed in any game all season. And when John Kitna's pass, with one minute and eight seconds remaining in the game, sailed past his tight end, Matt Schobel, and came to rest in a Browns defender's arms, the visitors sealed a 22–14 victory. No playoffs. No fairy-tale ending.

With both a gut-wrenchingly painful game and a sensationally groundbreaking season suddenly over, however, Lewis continued to lead. He stayed balanced, getting neither too low nor too high, and offered a simple workmanlike reflection: "This was a good year. It wasn't a great year. We've got more to do." All season, even when his troops were winless, he had implored them to "keep chopping." "Keep chopping," he promised, "and pretty soon that tree will fall." The off-season represented an opportunity to "keep chopping" toward the playoffs, and Lewis was ready to get started. By any objective assessment, Lewis' coaching performance during the 2003 season was impressive, and in NFL coach-of-the-year voting he finished second only to Bill Belichick, who had somehow rustled fourteen regular-season wins out of his chronically injured New England Patriots roster.

Back in December 2002 Lewis had been hoping he would one day be an NFL head coach, and the Bengals, desperate for an effective head coach, had never in their history considered anyone who looked like him for the position. A year later, Lewis' Bengals were a playoff contender and Lewis had earned his place among the League's best head coaches. He had arrived, as had the Rooney Rule. Even among many skeptics, Lewis' success validated the rule, and when seven of the League's thirty-two teams launched head coaching searches after the 2003 season's completion, each of them fully complied, and two of the seven hired African American head coaches. The Arizona Cardinals hired Dennis Green, the afterthought in Jerry Jones' Bill Parcells quest the previous year, and the Chicago Bears hired Lovie Smith, the St. Louis Rams' defensive coordinator and Tony Dungy mentee, who had never before the rule's implementation been invited to interview for a head coaching position. Together with Dungy, Edwards, and Lewis, Green and Smith raised the number of NFL head coaches of color to an all-time high of five.

Having successfully advocated for diverse candidate slates in the coaching context, the FPA, during the 2003 season, increasingly turned its attention to teams' front offices, which were even more homogenous than their coaching staffs. Recognizing that women of all races, like men of color, were struggling to access front office opportunity, the FPA urged the League to implement a modified Rooney Rule, which would require that teams interview a person of color or a woman before hiring a front office executive. The League was pleased with the Rooney Rule's impact, and while it stopped short of a mandate, it issued front office hiring guidelines recommending what the FPA proposed. There was no penalty attached for noncompliance, but it was a start and the FPA applauded it, all the while pushing the League for a firmer commitment.

What Mehri and Cochran had begun as a hopeful project two years earlier was now a full-fledged movement. Sadly, Cochran's participation in that movement was nearing its end.

10

DIGGING NEW WELLS

As Lewis marched his team through the 2003 season, the FPA steadily solidified its relationship with the NFL, the core of which was the relationship between Wooten and Goodell. The two had known each other for twenty years, and each sincerely respected and liked the other. Although Mehri and Pash's relationship did not enjoy the same decades-long foundation, they had developed a similarly strong connection. So when League officials encountered issues involving race, they consulted the FPA, and if during the coaching carousel the FPA suspected a team might violate the Rooney Rule or otherwise thwart the NFL's equal opportunity efforts, it notified the League. In addition, the FPA regularly provided the League with lists of coaches it deemed prepared for coordinator and head coaching positions so the League would be able to forward the list to teams claiming inability to identify qualified candidates of color. The two organizations had formed a partnership unlike any other in sport.

It seemed inconceivable that just over a year earlier Cochran had brazenly threatened litigation. Mehri smiled when he thought about how far his and Cochran's project had come since that press conference at Shula's, and he wished Cochran were still as involved as he once had been.

As the 2003 season wound down, Cochran's involvement in FPA affairs markedly declined. Initially it appeared that Cochran's frantic schedule was pulling him away, but Cochran soon informed Mehri there was more—some medical issues were temporarily sidetracking him. Since shortly after they met in 2001, the two had spoken almost every Monday morning to catch up and coordinate their calendars, and suddenly those calls stopped. Because Cochran had not indicated the issues were serious, Mehri was not terribly concerned, but he was sad. The two had accomplished so much with their NFL project that he wished Cochran were around more to enjoy the fruits of their labor. His sadness extended beyond that, though. In short, he missed his friend.

Before Cochran began withdrawing from the FPA, Mehri had hoped Cochran would deliver the keynote address when the FPA gathered at the 2004 Scouting Combine to celebrate the organization's successes and prospectively strategize. Mehri believed the honor of delivering the address would be a fitting tribute to Cochran; he also felt that Cochran would be able to motivate the FPA's members in a way nobody else could. With Cochran unavailable, however, the FPA had to look elsewhere for a speaker. Mehri, Wooten, and Winslow wanted someone who was familiar with the FPA and with its work, but also with the broader battle for racial equality in sports. After some deliberation, they settled on Ken Shropshire, a professor in the Legal Studies and Business Ethics Department of the University of Pennsylvania's Wharton School of Business. In Cochran's absence, Shropshire seemed the perfect choice.

Shropshire was a commanding speaker and, having authored numerous articles and books about the intersection of race and sports, he knew the terrain as well as anyone. But he was not just a scholar. He had lived what he was now writing and teaching. Years earlier he had played football on scholarship at Stanford University, where there were no African Americans on the coaching staff or in the athletic department's administration when he arrived. And he watched as his African American teammates, most of whom played quarterback in high school, were shifted at Stanford to other positions because the quarterback position was perennially occupied by whites. Shropshire ultimately experienced greater academic success than athletic success at Stanford, so as some teammates were launching their NFL careers, he enrolled at Columbia Law School still smarting from the inequities he had observed and experienced as a part of the Stanford football program. After graduating from law school, he returned to sports, representing players as an agent and serving on the 1984 Los Angeles Olympic Organizing Committee, all with an eye toward attendant racial dynamics.

A few years later, in 1987, Shropshire stumbled upon his first bona fide opportunity to directly aid the struggle for racial equity in sport. On April 6 of that year, ABC's *Nightline* television program aired an episode dedicated to commemorating Jackie Robinson's role in integrating Major League Baseball forty years earlier. As part of the show, Ted Koppel interviewed the Los Angeles Dodgers' general manager, Al Campanis. Robinson, of course, spent his entire major league career with the Dodgers, so the Campanis interview had all the makings of a nostalgic, feel-good jaunt. When Koppel probed Campanis as to why Major League Baseball had no African American managers or general managers, however, a disconcerting and at times bizarre exchange ensued:

CAMPANIS: I don't believe it's prejudice. I truly believe that
    they may not have some of the necessities to be, let's say,
    a field manger or perhaps a general manager.
KOPPEL: Do you really believe that?
CAMPANIS: Well, I don't say that all of them, but they
    certainly are short. How many quarterbacks do you have,
    how many pitchers do you have, that are black?
KOPPEL: Yeah, but I got to tell you, that sounds like the
    same kind of garbage we were hearing 40 years ago about
    players.

CAMPANIS: No, it's not garbage, Mr. Koppel, because I played on a college team, and the center-fielder was black, and in the backfield at NYU with a fullback who was black. Never knew the difference whether he was black or white. We were teammates. So it might just be, why are black men or black people not good swimmers? Because they don't have buoyancy.

After a commercial break, Koppel offered Campanis an opportunity to clarify his comments. Campanis tried, but he could not. His view of African Americans' intellectual capacities was too deeply set. He simply could not break from it. Instead, he lauded African Americans' athletic abilities, gushing, "They are gifted with great musculature and various other things [and] they're fleet of foot." Ultimately, though, he circled back to where he had begun: "Now as far as having the background to become club presidents or presidents of banks . . . I don't know."

Koppel got his answer, although not in the manner he expected. Major League Baseball did not have any African American managers or general managers because of stereotypes such as those Campanis so comfortably asserted as fact.

Outrage ensued, and two days later the Dodgers fired Campanis. The termination did little to calm incensed members of the public or console African American former major leaguers who had been trying desperately to acquire the very positions for which Campanis matter-of-factly declared them unfit. While it was not shocking to learn that a high-ranking baseball executive held such views, it was shocking to hear them so forthrightly expressed. It was particularly shocking because Campanis was reputedly fair-minded. Indeed, Don Newcombe, an African American pitcher who had played many seasons for the Dodgers, once described Campanis as not having "a prejudiced bone in his body."

If Marge Schott—then owner, president, and CEO of the Cincinnati Reds, and who later allegedly would describe two of her best players as "million-dollar niggers" and insist she would "rather have a trained monkey working for [her] than a nigger"—had answered Koppel's questions as Campanis did, the comments would have been less startling. But if Campanis, who had not previously revealed himself as a racist, harbored such prejudices, so too potentially might every executive in the league.

Current and retired African American major leaguers rallied in response to Campanis' comments, and they sought help from Stanford law professor William Gould, a nationally renowned sports law expert. Gould, unavailable at the time to assist them, recommended his former student and mentee, Shropshire, who had just joined the Wharton faculty. Within days Shropshire was on the phone with Willie Stargell, the great Pittsburgh Pirates first baseman, who since retiring had grown increasingly frustrated with the baseball community's seeming unwillingness to consider people of color for authoritative off-field positions. Stargell invited Shropshire to a meeting he was organizing in Dallas, and Shropshire accepted. At that meeting Stargell, along with Frank Robinson, Bob Watson, Don Baylor, Dusty Baker, Dave Winfield, and other legendary players of color, shared, sometimes through tears, the mistreatment and discrimination they had suffered at the hands of their teams and Major League Baseball. Many had attempted to stay in baseball as scouts, managers, or front office executives but were flatly denied opportunities. That day, the players and former players committed to work as a unit in seeking equal opportunity in baseball.

Over the course of two years, with Shropshire representing them, the Baseball Network, as the organization came to be called, met with Major League Baseball's commissioner and his management team on several occasions to apprise them of the untapped managerial talent among former players of color and to push for increased attention to diversity. Major League Baseball responded by expanding equal opportunity, and people of color began appearing in teams' dugouts as managers and in their front offices as executives. Such rapid progress would have been unlikely without the Network's effort, and Shropshire was a substantial contributor to that effort.

The FPA was working to do for football what the Baseball Network had done for baseball fifteen years earlier. Mehri, Wooten, and Winslow believed Shropshire's Baseball Network–related knowledge, together with the expertise he had developed during the decade and a half since his work with the Network, might aid the FPA's endeavors and serve to inspire its members. Shropshire agreed to deliver the keynote address in the Indianapolis Hyatt's Harrison Conference Room on the Combine's second day.

As close as Shropshire had been to the game of football, as a player and then as an agent, since entering academia he had grown apart from the game and its rhythm, a fundamental feature of which is early morning activity. Most coaches are up, about, and hard at work by 6:30 a.m. Six o'clock thus seemed to Wooten and Winslow a natural time to schedule the organization's Combine gathering—so natural, in fact, that when they invited Shropshire to participate and asked that he be ready to speak on February 19 by six o'clock, they neglected to specify morning rather than evening. So when Shropshire telephoned Winslow from Philadelphia around noon on the eighteenth to say his flight would arrive in Indianapolis by three in the afternoon, Winslow's retort—"Well, you better hurry up and get to the airport"—made no sense.

"No, I mean three o'clock tomorrow," stated Shropshire, still confused.

"Then you'll miss the meeting," Winslow responded, trying to conceal his amusement at what he suddenly realized was Shropshire's error.

The professor, embarrassed, scrambled to rebook his flight for that evening and arrived at the Indianapolis Hyatt late that night, giving him only a few hours of sleep before he was scheduled to speak. On most days Shropshire's wife, an anesthesiologist, left home by 6:00 a.m., so despite Shropshire's flexible academic schedule, he was by necessity an early riser. He generally dedicated the period between his wife's departure and the time at which his children awoke to quiet relaxation, however, and orating at such an early hour, particularly on short sleep, would prove a challenge. But the remarks he planned to deliver meant a great deal to him, and he resolved to do his best.

The FPA's 2004 Combine meeting was drastically different from the one the organization had held the year before. This time around, there was no fear in the room. Heads had not rolled. In fact, nobody in the organization had suffered any retaliation for his involvement. Rather than worry about their job security, members ate breakfast and chatted cheerfully, knowing that through the organization they had strengthened their collective status. The meeting's formal program further enhanced the room's festive atmosphere. The group celebrated the late Tank Younger, who before passing away in 2001 had done so much to lay the foundation for what would become the FPA, and Wooten and Winslow presented Tony Dungy and Frank Gilliam with awards for all of their work over the years to advance the cause of African Americans in the NFL. In addition, Mehri presented an award to Janice Madden for her statistical analysis, which essentially had launched the movement of which all in the room were now a part.

When Shropshire, still a bit bleary-eyed, approached the microphone to deliver his address, he took a different tone. He was as excited about the FPA's progress as everyone else, and he followed that progress with satisfaction and pride, knowing the FPA was taking the Baseball Network's ideas and efforts to the next level. Moreover, Shropshire recognized that the FPA's power was only increasing. He wanted to use his time at the podium to urge reflection and vision creation.

"We drink from wells we did not dig," Shropshire began, letting the sentence hang for a few moments before continuing. He then recounted the story of Moses "Fleetwood" Walker, an African American catcher in America's fledgling professional baseball leagues during the late 1880s, before baseball segregated and then reintegrated a half century later. When Walker played, he was almost always the lone African American on the field, and throughout his career, he endured untold racially motivated mistreatment. "No wells had been dug to ease Walker's thirst," Shropshire told the audience, which was attentive from his first few words. "He dug on his own." Next Shropshire spoke about the organization's namesake, detailing the ugly repression Fritz Pollard suffered while playing and coaching during the 1920s. Walker, Pollard, and the other African American pioneers of early American sport, Shropshire intoned, "excelled and survived, so others could follow. They dug the wells that we all, to varying degrees, enjoy."

Shropshire was teaching now, and after a few more comments about the discrimination that had long racked American sports and American society in general, he swung his lecture in a seemingly unrelated direction, as he might back at Wharton in order to coax a classroom of students toward a larger point. He began talking about Alfred B. Nobel, a prolific nineteenth-century inventor who held more than 350 patents, the most famous of which was for dynamite.

According to legend, Shropshire asserted, when Alfred Nobel's brother died, a newspaper mistakenly printed an obituary it had prepared in anticipation of Alfred's death, giving Alfred the surreal opportunity to read what others thought of him. What he read was devastating. The obituary distinguished him as the man who created a product capable of killing more people at once than anything previously existent. Alfred was in actuality a poetry-loving pacifist who invented dynamite with an eye toward its peaceful uses, and he could not bear to be remembered for creating a weapon of war. So in his will Alfred Nobel directed that much of his expansive fortune be used to fund a number of annual prizes, including the Nobel Peace Prize.

With that, Shropshire circled back to the men in the room and their organization.

"It is not often that someone gets the chance to rewrite their legacy once it has been set. But we all have the opportunity to establish it in the first place. Tonight—not to be morbid; let's all say our prayers and then afterward—take your best mental shot at writing your own obituary. If you end with 'great coach, wonderful father,' that is reason for pride. If you want more and you haven't taken a step in the right direction, think of the Nobel story. Think of your possible role in this struggle. Are you going to drink from the well or dig new and deeper wells?"

Shropshire closed his remarks with a few final comments, but his challenge lingered in the room, almost eclipsing the words that followed. As Shropshire stepped away from the podium and FPA members pounded out applause, each had to grapple with Shropshire's question: was he digging or simply drinking? As with any organization, some FPA members were more involved than others. Some worked along with the organization's leaders, while others were more passive, enjoying the sweet taste of formerly inaccessible opportunity on the strength of others' efforts. The latter were drinking without digging, and Shropshire was challenging them.

Shropshire's bigger challenge was geared toward the FPA as a whole. In one year, the organization had altered NFL-wide head coach hiring practices and spurred increased diversity among teams' coaching staffs. The organization's progress was stunning, and because it had accomplished so much so quickly, Shropshire believed it was capable of far more. Looking back, Shropshire regretted that the Baseball Network never fully recognized the power it held. He did not want the individuals assembled before him to have similar regrets one day.

Some motivational speeches are sufficiently general that the identity of the speaker is almost irrelevant to the speech's efficacy. Others are so personal and penetrating that the manner in which they are received depends largely on the individual giving them. Shropshire's speech was in the latter group. Delivered by someone else, his remarks might have had no appreciable impact. Shropshire had been fighting discrimination in the sports industry for two decades, yet with his comments he seemed to be challenging himself as much as anyone else in the room. If he was not above introspection, they had to ask themselves, why should they be? Ultimately they weren't, individually or collectively. Nobody could dispute the debt the FPA and its members owed to Walker, Pollard, and others who had fought the first battles for African American inclusion in sports. Nor could anybody repay it. In his speech, Shropshire emphasized what everyone, on some level, knew: they had inherited fully formed wells and with them the responsibility to dig new ones.

The 2004 Combine meeting invigorated the already surging FPA, and in the meeting's wake, the FPA's leadership began considering how and where it might most effectively dig. With Cochran still out of touch, it seemed they would have to dig without him, and, if necessary, they were prepared to do so. But they would soon learn precisely why Cochran had not been around.

The FPA's leadership had begun to quietly conclude, based on the length of Cochran's absence and silence, that the medical issues he mentioned to Mehri were more serious than he had initially indicated. They knew something was wrong, but they did not know what. Virtually no one did. Cochran had kept the nature and severity of his ailment under wraps, revealing his condition only to some family members and his law firm partners. Even his mother-in-law was in the dark.

It turned out that back in December 2003, doctors had detected a malignant tumor in Cochran's brain. Almost immediately Cochran retreated into seclusion, not just from the FPA but from virtually everybody in his life, to protect both his privacy and his law firm, which drew much of its prestige and business from his name and reputation.

In early April 2004 Cochran finally publicly revealed his condition, and just a few days later surgeons operated. Initially the procedure appeared successful. Cochran spent three postoperative weeks in the hospital and then several additional months recovering at home, and by the fall of 2004 he proclaimed himself 90 percent recovered and was planning to significantly expand his practice. Aside from slightly slurred speech, he had seemingly overcome the ordeal, and doctors were predicting he would be back to his old self by year's end. Unfortunately, Cochran's condition worsened, and he slid back into seclusion. On March 29, 2005, almost a year after his surgery, he was dead.

In death, as he had in life, Cochran appeared mainly in one dimension, by virtue of the media's references to O. J. Simpson. Seemingly every print and broadcast story about Cochran's passing focused on the O.J. case, largely neglecting the rest of his career.

Those closest to Cochran, however, had a fuller picture of the man, and on April 6, 2005, they gathered at the West Angeles Cathedral in Los Angeles, California, to celebrate Cochran's life and mourn his death. The group included celebrity clients—Simpson, pop icon Michael Jackson, music mogul Sean Combs, and others—but also everyday citizens whose civil rights Cochran had zealously protected, such as the long-incarcerated Pratt and New York police brutality victim Abner Louima. And, of course, there were scores of nonclients, some famous, some not, all in attendance to offer their respects. Mehri was among them, as was Harry Carson, the former New York Giants linebacker and new FPA executive director.

In the fall of 2004, Winslow had stepped down as FPA executive director to become the director of planning and new event development with the Walt Disney Company's Sports and Recreation Division, and Carson agreed to replace him. Carson, like Winslow, was a natural leader, but with an entirely different style. Calm and calculating, Carson spoke and acted on an even keel, seeming never to raise his voice or even substantially inflect it. It was hard to believe he'd spent more than a decade's worth of autumn Sundays pulverizing opposing running backs or that he'd once executed an unthinkable twenty-five tackles in a single game. Carson's disposition seemed better suited to pediatrics than linebacking, but he had nevertheless compiled an impressive Hall of Fame–caliber playing career, after which, like Winslow, he focused on bolstering off-field football opportunities for people of color. Winslow's departure was a significant loss for the FPA, but Carson proved a strong replacement.

Cochran's memorial service was at once deeply touching and inspiring, and it served as a powerful rebuke to the professional typecasting Cochran had suffered. A parade of mourners, one after the next, shared with the assembled masses how Cochran had touched their lives. Charles J. Ogletree Jr. was among them, and although he took the opportunity to express what Cochran had meant to him personally, he was compelled to go further. He believed that everyone in the cathedral should know what Cochran meant to the civil rights community, and he felt duty-bound to tell them.

Ogletree did not enjoy the celebrity that characterized many of the others who eulogized Cochran that day, but by virtue of hard work and a razor-sharp intellect he had molded himself into, by most estimates, the best civil rights lawyer in the nation. Although he would shrink from the appellation if given a chance, it was hard to contest. Ogletree was a chaired professor at Harvard Law School and from that position made a career of targeting and attacking injustice. Before joining the Harvard faculty, Ogletree had established himself among the best public defenders at the District of Columbia Public Defender Service, ultimately rising to the deputy director position. Eventually he left that office to launch a private criminal defense practice. From there, Ogletree went to Harvard, where he committed himself to continuing the unfinished work of Charles Hamilton Houston, the brilliant litigator and scholar who had crafted the legal strategy that would culminate in the Supreme Court's *Brown v. Board* decision and who, throughout his career, challenged racial discrimination in all its forms.

Ogletree was indefatigable in his mission for equal justice, litigating cases, testifying before Congress, authoring articles and books, convening symposia, and teaching classes, all geared toward making America a more racially just society. Perhaps Ogletree's most ambitious project regarded an eighty-year-old race riot of which few Americans were aware. In the early 1900s, when virulent racial discrimination dominated the American landscape, an extraordinary African American business and residential community, known as "Negro Wall Street," managed to flourished in the Greenwood section of Tulsa, Oklahoma. Replete with commercial enterprises of all sorts, lawyers' and doctors' officers, a hospital, two high schools, and several hotels, Greenwood was wildly prosperous and entirely self-sufficient, ultimately sparking envy among its white neighbors.

On May 30, 1921, in Tulsa, a young African American man named Dick Rowland accidentally fell onto and grabbed a white female elevator operator named Sarah Page. Page screamed that she was being attacked, and, fearing he would be falsely accused of sexual assault—an entirely rational fear in light of the era's racial dynamics—Rowland ran out of the elevator when the doors opened. Several white men saw Rowland run, and the next day, what Rowland had feared came to pass and he was arrested. Once word of the incident spread, a mob of thousands descended on the jail in which he was being held, with plans to lynch him.

In hopes of preventing the young man's murder, nearly a hundred armed African American Greenwood residents arrived at the jail that evening to assist the sheriff in holding off the mob. The sheriff convinced them he would protect Rowland, and the Greenwood residents began to disperse. But as they did, a white man, enraged at the African Americans' audacity, demanded that one of the Greenwood residents surrender his gun. The latter refused, and the former lunged for the weapon, which discharged.

Within moments guns were firing in all directions, and as the violence escalated, some Tulsa policemen began deputizing any whites willing to join the fight, urging them to "get a gun and get a nigger." Shortly thereafter, the National Guard joined in, ostensibly to squelch what quickly became known as the "Negro Uprising." By morning, swarms of white rioters, with law officers and National Guardsmen joining the fray, invaded Greenwood on foot, in automobiles, and, astoundingly, with airplanes, systematically destroying the thriving community.

The attackers generally looted the buildings first, taking what they wanted, and then torched them. Along the way, they wantonly terrorized Greenwood citizens, either shooting or incinerating those who resisted. It was a gruesome and criminal massacre, and, unbelievably, at the turn of the millennium hardly anyone in the country knew anything about it. Ogletree set out to change that, organizing many of the nation's most talented and progressive lawyers and scholars into what became the Reparations Coordinating Committee (RCC) and in 2003 bringing suit on behalf of the riot's survivors and the descendants of those who had died in the violence.

Johnnie Cochran was among the RCC's members. Ogletree would not have had it any other way. Ogletree had admired Cochran since the former was a Stanford University undergraduate student and knew Cochran only as the "young and talented southern California lawyer who represented the nameless, faceless, and powerless individuals in and around Los Angeles."

Ogletree, 350 miles up the California coast, followed Cochran's career through news reports and was impressed by Cochran's willingness to represent brutality victims against the mighty Los Angeles Police Department. "It was clear then," Ogletree would later recall, "that while the black community felt they had no one to protect their life and liberty from police misconduct here was somebody not afraid to stand up to the police and not afraid to represent poor black people."

Cochran struck Ogletree as the type of lawyer he would one day want to be, and when Ogletree, by then a Harvard Law School student, met Cochran in person, it only confirmed his impression. Later, once Ogletree began practicing law, the two lawyers found themselves, on different occasions, as both co-counsel and opposing counsel, and they developed a sincere and profound mutual respect.

Suddenly, though, the man who had inspired Ogletree decades earlier and who then became Ogletree's colleague and friend was gone, and, standing before thousands of fellow mourners in the massive West Angeles Cathedral, Ogletree wanted them to know the lawyer they had lost. Ogletree's eulogy was the sort of oration felt more than heard, characterized less by words and phrases than by the spirit in which it was delivered. His ultimate message, though, was simple: "Johnnie represented not only the O.J.'s but the A.J.'s, B.J.'s, C.J.'s, and P.J.'s—the unknowns in our community—on a pro bono basis. His epitaph should say, 'When people called, Johnnie would come.'"

Although the FPA would have to press on without Cochran's involvement, the foundation Cochran had helped create was strong. During the few years it had been in existence, the organization had grown dramatically in repute and influence, and, inspired by Shropshire's exhortation, it gradually began expanding its initiatives, working toward securing equal opportunity for people of color aspiring to be NFL game-day officials and NCAA Division I football head coaches. In addition, in 2006 the FPA established a program to recognize and encourage academically and athletically outstanding high school football players, and during Super Bowl week in 2007 the selected students joined the FPA and its members for an awards ceremony named in Cochran's honor and held in Miami, where the game would be played. The Johnnie L. Cochran Jr. Salute to Excellence Awards reception, at which both the students and the season's most successful coaches and general managers of color received commendations, provided the students an opportunity to rub shoulders with their heroes and provided their heroes an opportunity to mentor.

Gathering together to celebrate one another, honor Cochran, and applaud the youngsters was an exhilarating and emotional experience for all in attendance. Two members of the organization, however, were conspicuously absent, choosing to forgo the fellowship and camaraderie the others were enjoying, but no one in the room begrudged them. By all accounts, they had more important things to do.

11

THE ROAD TO SUPER BOWL XLI

Tony Dungy's Indianapolis Colts had ended their 2005 season in surreally disastrous fashion. After winning fourteen of their sixteen regular-season games, the Colts entered the postseason as the AFC's top-seeded team and were the prohibitive Super Bowl favorites. The Colts' first playoff opponent was the Pittsburgh Steelers, and virtually everyone expected the Colts to win. The Steelers were the sixth and final team in the AFC to qualify for the playoffs, and since 1990, when the NFL expanded its playoff system to include six teams from each conference, no sixth seed had ever defeated a first seed. Even though the Steelers were surging, having won their final four regular-season games as well as the previous week's first-round playoff game against the Cincinnati Bengals, an upset in Indianapolis was not likely. Indeed, while the Steelers were battling the Bengals, the Colts, by virtue of their first-round playoff bye, were recuperating from the physical toll of the season and were as healthy and rested as a group of football players could expect to be after sixteen punishing NFL games.

There was one particularly notable and bizarre exception, however: starting Colts cornerback Nick Harper had spent a portion of the day before the game at the hospital courtesy of his wife, Daniell, and a fillet knife. The Harpers' marriage, at least according to the police blotter, was a mess. Just a few months earlier, authorities had arrested Nick for assaulting Daniell. This time it was Daniell's turn. Frustrated that Nick was refusing to speak to her, she menacingly waved the utensil above him as he lay in their bed and then plunged it an inch into his right knee.

Although Harper required multiple stitches, the blade did not sever any ligaments, and despite initial uncertainty as to whether Harper would be capable of taking the field with his fresh wound, by game time he proclaimed himself ready to play. The Colts, it appeared, would be no worse for wear. That is, until the game's final one minute and twenty seconds.

Nursing a 21–18 lead, with the ball at the Colts' two-yard line and four downs with which to work, the Steelers were on the brink of victory, and their head coach, Bill Cowher, sent running back Jerome Bettis into the game to finish the Colts off. Nicknamed "The Bus," Bettis matched the moniker. He was a hulking, bruising runner, perfectly designed for goal-line situations. Moreover, he wasn't likely to fumble; he had not done so all year. So when the Steelers called the safest play in their playbook—Counter 38 Power—and quarterback Ben Roethlisberger handed the ball to Bettis, who briefly cut to the right and then drove toward the end zone, a Steelers victory seemed inevitable. But then Colts linebacker Gary Brackett imposed his will, blasting Bettis at the goal line and jarring the ball free.

From a frantic montage of the Colts' blue and white, the Steelers' white, black, and yellow, and the green RCA Dome turf, a bluish blur emerged with the ball and began running in the other direction toward the most improbable of touchdowns and a certain berth for the Colts in the AFC Championship Game. The ball carrier was the freshly sutured Nick Harper, and in an instant it was clear that he had only Roethlisberger, who was stumbling and falling backward, to beat. Running toward Roethlisberger, Harper cut left, pushing off his wounded right leg. The quarterback lunged, grabbing just enough of that right leg to fell Harper on the Colts' forty-two-yard line. There would be no touchdown for Harper, and in the game's last minute the Colts' offense would prove incapable of converting the turnover into points. The Colts' season was over, and the Steelers would go on to win the Super Bowl.

Perhaps an uninjured Harper would have fared exactly the same against the diving Roethlisberger. It was possible, though, that Harper's stab wound made the difference between an early playoff exit and another step toward the Super Bowl. There was no way to know for sure, which produced an unsettling anxiety among Colts fans throughout the spring and summer of 2006. But the team itself, under Dungy's command, showed no sign of adopting a defeatist, snake-bitten mentality, and when the 2006 season began they won their first nine games and finished the season 12–4. Rather than the AFC's first playoff seed, which they had had in 2005, however, their record was good enough only for the third seed, which meant no first-round bye.

In their first-round game, less than twenty-four hours after Dungy, Herman Edwards, and Lovie Smith enjoyed the rare opportunity to share fellowship over a meal, Dungy's Colts defeated Edwards' Chiefs. A week later, after escaping Baltimore and its venom-spewing Ravens fans with a hard-earned victory, Dungy and his Colts were one game away from the Super Bowl.

Smith and his Chicago Bears were similarly situated. The day after the Colts beat the Ravens, the Bears, the NFC's best team during the regular season, hosted and defeated the Seattle Seahawks, 27–24. The following Sunday, January 21, Dungy and Smith would coach in their respective conference's championship games, giving each the chance to be the first African American head coach in NFL history to reach the sport's summit and providing the possibility that the two friends would reach it together.

In four different rooms in three different cities, Mehri, Wooten, Carson, and Winslow awoke on the twenty-first with the same feeling: anxious excitement. Winslow had long left the FPA, but he remained faithfully connected to the group and its cause. Moreover, like Wooten, Mehri, Carson, and anyone else who had spent time with Dungy and Smith, Winslow knew that both were quality individuals, and he wished the best for them.

Dungy's reputation as a kind and decent man had spread widely over the course of the previous few years, but Smith, although less heralded in that respect, was no less kind or decent. He carried himself humbly and treated others as he would want to be treated, as one fan in the RCA Dome two weeks earlier had learned. Smith, having decided to stay in Indianapolis beyond dinner and attend the Chiefs-Colts game, found himself torn between watching his buddies' teams battle for their playoff lives and satisfying the autograph seekers who seemed unaware or unconcerned that their requests might distract him from the nuances of the game he so desperately wanted to track.

After signing for some time, Smith returned his focus to the match in which Dungy and Edwards were engaged. When another fan approached him, Smith politely declined to sign, explaining his desire to concentrate on the game. For most celebrity sports figures, the interaction would have ended there. Smith, by contrast, carefully noted the seat to which the fan returned, and when there was a break in the action, he left his seat, walked over to hers, and signed.

Putting color aside, Dungy and Smith were top-notch coaches and top-notch human beings, the type of people for whom one instinctively roots. But Mehri, Wooten, Carson, and Winslow knew that color could not be put aside. The stunted careers of African American head coaching aspirants splayed out across the NFL's historic landscape made it impossible. The time had come for an African American to lead a football team, the most complex of American sporting operations, to the sport's apex. Until it happened, many Americans would believe it never could.

So Mehri in D.C., Winslow in Orlando, Florida, and Wooten and Carson in Mobile, Alabama, for the Senior Bowl knew January 21, 2007, was no ordinary day, and each spent it watching a lot of football.

Smith's Bears played first, hosting the surprising New Orleans Saints at Chicago's Soldier Field. Before the season, only a lunatic would have predicted a Saints appearance in the NFC Championship. More famous for their embarrassing nickname, the "New Orleans Ain'ts," than for their on-field performance, the Saints had never been to a conference championship game since their 1967 founding. The weight of that history, though, was nothing compared with the weight of daily life in their city.

Just a year and a half earlier, during the 2005 NFL preseason, a storm brewed over the Bahamas, was given the name Katrina, and developed into a mammoth hurricane. It pounded New Orleans, a city situated several feet below sea level, into submission. Hurricane Katrina killed nearly two thousand people, displaced hundreds of thousands more, and flooded 80 percent of the city. Many of the displaced never returned, opting to begin new lives on higher ground, and the city had become a shell of its former self, struggling to survive. Those who remained and those who returned clung to the Saints as a temporary distraction from the tragedy.

As hard as the Saints tried during that 2005 season, however, the team was unable to overcome the challenges Katrina presented. The Saints' stadium, the Louisiana Superdome, which had sheltered more than thirty thousand New Orleanians during the storm, had not been able to entirely withstand its fury. A piece of the roof gave way, and the resulting damage made the Saints' home field unplayable. Consequently, the team played both its home games and away games during the 2005 season on the road. They played one "home" game against the New York Giants at Giants Stadium, and they played the rest either in San Antonio, Texas, at the Alamodome or at Louisiana State University's Tiger Stadium. Nobody expected a successful season, and the Saints, who won only three games, did not deliver one.

In 2006, back in the Superdome, the Saints embarked on a season for the ages, fueling the collective spirit of a city still struggling to rebuild. With ten regular-season wins, the Saints made the playoffs for only the seventh time in franchise history and, with a 27–24 playoff victory over the Philadelphia Eagles, were enjoying their best-ever season.

When the Saints arrived in Chicago, they were the undisputed sentimental favorite, and because they had the League's top-rated offense, led by their dynamic quarterback, Drew Brees, many pundits picked them to win. The Chicago winter, however, rose up to defend its Bears. The Saints, accustomed to the climate-controlled Superdome and heavily reliant on passing the ball, were not used to playing in the snow or extreme cold, and the cloudy Chicago afternoon during which the two teams met for the right to represent the NFC in the Super Bowl offered both.

Smith took advantage of the weather, centering his strategy around running the football and avoiding costly mistakes, and his players faithfully executed his game plan. Aside from a brief moment during the fourth quarter when the Saints pulled within two points, the outcome was never in doubt, and when time expired, the score was Chicago 39, New Orleans 14. The Bears were bound for the Super Bowl.

In the Colts' locker room, while preparing for his own game, Dungy watched portions of the Bears' victory and swelled with pride at the way Smith's team played. When Dungy saw that the Bears had taken an eighteen-point lead, he was certain they would win. "That's three scores," he thought. "This game's over." As Dungy left the locker room and walked out to the field to observe his players warming up, he never imagined his team would soon be trailing by exactly that margin.

Everybody in Indianapolis, including Dungy and his players, knew that despite the Colts' higher playoff seed and their home field advantage, the AFC Championship Game against the New England Patriots would be an immense challenge. The Patriots, who had won three of the previous five Super Bowls, were the Colts' nemesis, always seeming to beat them in the big games. Although the Colts had won the teams' regular-season meeting, the Patriots tended to play their best football in the postseason; in fact, the Patriots' coach, Bill Belichick, and their starting quarterback, Tom Brady, had never lost a conference championship game.

Still, nobody expected the Patriots to storm out to a 21–3 lead, the same score differential Dungy had hours earlier deemed insurmountable. Any student of NFL history would have concurred with Dungy's assessment, as no NFL team had ever overcome such a deficit in a conference championship game. But when faced with the deficit himself, Dungy found that it did not seem so hopeless. In fact, following New England's extra-point conversion, which extended the lead from seventeen to eighteen points, Dungy walked over to his offensive unit, which was assembled on the sideline, and issued a simple message: "We're going to win this game." Dungy did not yell, melt down, or put his finger in anybody's face. He simply told his players what he believed. The Colts' offense was powerful and could score in bunches, and the team had overcome large deficits in the past. If Dungy kept his players focused and composed, he knew, they could prevail.

He was right. The Colts scored the next eighteen points to tie the game, and after trading the lead throughout the fourth quarter, the Colts scored the game's last touchdown to open a 38–34 lead. The Patriots had one last offensive opportunity, but when Colts defender Marlin Jackson intercepted a Brady pass with sixteen seconds remaining and dropped down to the turf cradling the ball, it was over. The Colts had beaten history and punched the second and final ticket to Super Bowl XLI, meaning that Dungy, whose mistreatment had catalyzed Mehri and Cochran to propose what became the Rooney Rule and to help found the FPA, and Smith, a beneficiary of both, would meet two weeks later for NFL supremacy.

Over the course of several years Dungy and Smith, both class acts, had crafted exceptional football teams through meticulous preparation and instruction and through inspiring respect rather than fear in their players. And in one extraordinary season they both made all the right calls: when to go for it on fourth down and when to punt; when to settle for an extra point and when to attempt a two-point conversion; when to push players harder and when to insist they rest. They masterminded their respective teams' successes and were both, finally, conference champions.

In postgame comments, both coaches explained the importance their victories held not just for their franchises and their cities but also for African Americans. "It means a lot," Dungy acknowledged when asked about the day's racial significance. "I'm very proud to be representing African Americans." Smith, after expressing the same sentiment, went a step further, taking a playful jab at his friend: "I'll feel even better to be the first black coach to hold up the world championship trophy." It was a reminder that neither coach's job was complete: there remained one game to play, and on February 1, 2007, while their friends and colleagues were enjoying the Salute to Excellence Awards reception, Dungy and Smith were busily preparing for that game. To those who had gathered to celebrate the FPA and fete the Super Bowl coaches in absentia, however, the game's outcome meant little. They had all already won.

EPILOGUE

IN EARLY 2002, BEFORE CRAFTING AN ACTION PLAN, commissioning a statistical study, or threatening the NFL, Cyrus Mehri and Johnnie Cochran feared what a few dozen white men leading thousands of mostly African American men into weekly physical competition meant to America. They cringed at the subtle notions they imagined it prompted among the football-watching populace—suppositions about intelligence, poise, and leadership ability that had long under-girded American racial discrimination.

On February 4, 2007, as Tony Dungy and Lovie Smith led their respective teams onto the field for Super Bowl XLI, Mehri, and perhaps Cochran looking down on it all, pondered a different, vastly more enjoyable question: what did two African Americans coaching against each other in the nation's premier athletic contest mean?

It certainly meant that when Tony Dungy signed a football for an African American child, adding the words "Follow your dream!" after his signature, the child knew Dungy had achieved his dream, and that, whatever the obstacles, the child could do the same. And it certainly further validated the NFL's Rooney Rule, which by Smith's admission had helped propel him into his head coaching position with the Bears. In addition, it was a testament to collective action. The NFL's off-field African Americans had accomplished more together than they could have as individuals. They prevailed over fear to become the Fritz Pollard Alliance, and as members of the FPA, they protected and empowered each other.

Above all else, Super Bowl XLI spoke to the importance of opportunity and the danger of myopia, not just as a matter of equity but as a matter of business. For the Colts and the Bears, success meant marching toward the 2007 Super Bowl. Dungy and Smith molded their teams in their own image—calm, composed, indomitable—and led those teams to conference championships, outpacing and defeating their competitors. Had the Colts and Bears clung to old stereotypes long pervading their industry, they would have deprived themselves of Dungy's and Smith's services and the success they spawned. Instead, those clubs transcended the stereotypes, and they profited.

Organizations unrelated to the NFL had begun taking notice of the League's changing complexion before the historic Dungy-Smith Super Bowl, but that game proved a watershed moment.

The Association of Art Museum Directors, for instance, knowing that Richard Lapchick had been involved in the NFL's equal opportunity movement, approached him with questions about the Rooney Rule in hopes that a similar rule might assist in diversifying the leadership ranks of the nation's art museums. And the National Urban League, inspired by the Rooney Rule's success, approached the NFL directly to learn more about diverse candidate slates so as to recommend them as a means of increasing equal employment opportunity throughout the business community.

Even the NCAA, in which aspiring football head coaches of color continued to flounder even more helplessly than aspiring head coaches of color in the NFL once had, seemed moved by the Dungy-Smith Super Bowl. For years the FPA had pressed the NCAA to urge its member institutions to implement diverse candidate slates in conducting head football coach searches, but the NCAA had been resistant. Finally, in 2007 the Division I-A Athletic Directors' Association began seriously contemplating the benefits diverse candidate slates might hold for college football. And in early 2008 it issued guidelines strongly encouraging the nation's Football Bowl Subdivision programs (known until 2006 as Division I-A football programs) to utilize such slates in hiring head football coaches. Believing that neither it nor the NCAA had the authority to mandate implementation, the Athletic Directors' Association attached no penalties for noncompliance. Nevertheless, Dutch Baughman, the association's executive director, implored his membership to comply, and athletic directors began utilizing diverse candidate slates during their football head coach searches. In short order, the number of Football Bowl Subdivision head coaches of color began to rise, and after the 2009 season it doubled from seven to fourteen.

Earlier that year, citing the Rooney Rule as its inspiration, the Oregon legislature took the efforts of the Athletic Directors' Association a step further, requiring that its seven public universities implement diverse candidate slates when searching for athletic directors as well as head coaches for all of their athletic programs. By the time the Oregon bill became law, Alabama state representative John Rogers had begun drafting a similar bill, which he planned to introduce in his state, one of the nation's football hotbeds. Whether Rogers would succeed was unknown, but the prospect of the University of Alabama, Auburn University, and the historically repressive state's other public institutions of higher education implementing diverse candidate slates as a matter of course was a delicious prospect for equal rights activists the nation over.

Just as the Rooney Rule's influence spread across the nation, its impact in the NFL continued to expand. In the midst of the Dungy-Smith Super Bowl run-up and surrounding fanfare, the Pittsburgh Steelers quietly worked toward hiring a new head coach. If not for what Dungy and Smith were accomplishing, the search would have been a far more substantial story than it was. The Steelers were arguably the most renowned franchise in League history and, along with the Dallas Cowboys, had won more Super Bowls than any other NFL team. Unlike the Cowboys under Jones, however, the Steelers rarely changed head coaches. Indeed, the most recent two, Chuck Noll and Bill Cowher, had led the team for a combined thirty-eight years.

So, whatever the surrounding circumstances, a Steelers head coach search was newsworthy. The circumstances in early 2007 made it far more so. The search represented the Rooney Rule coming full circle. Bill Cowher's January 5 resignation positioned Dan Rooney to effectuate the rule that bore his name. For the first time since the rule's enactment he had to walk his talk, and he did so. Rooney and his Steelers organization interviewed four candidates, two of whom were white and two of whom were of color.

The least heralded of the four was a young man named Mike Tomlin, who by all outside accounts stood absolutely no chance at the job. Consider the competition:

Ron Rivera, the Chicago Bears' defensive coordinator, had played nine seasons in the NFL with the Bears, winning one Super Bowl. A few years after retiring in 1992, he joined the Bears' coaching staff as a quality control assistant. From there he became the linebackers coach for the Philadelphia Eagles before returning to Chicago as the defensive coordinator in 2004.

Russ Grimm, a four-time Pro Bowl offensive guard who had won three Super Bowls with the Washington Redskins, coached the Redskins' tight ends from 1992 to 1996 and its offensive line from 1997 to 2000, after which he joined the Steelers as an offensive line coach. In 2004 the Steelers promoted Grimm to assistant head coach.

Ken Whisenhunt, like Grimm, was a Steelers coach. In 2001 he began coaching the team's tight ends and in 2004 became the Steelers' offensive coordinator. He too had enjoyed a long NFL career, playing for three different teams over the course of nine seasons.

Tomlin, by contrast, had never played in the NFL, and while he had played wide receiver on the collegiate level, he did so at lightly regarded William and Mary in the since disbanded Yankee Conference. Although he entered the NFL as a coach at the same time as Whisenhunt, in 2001, he had served as a coordinator with the

Minnesota Vikings for just one year when the Steelers' head coaching position opened up.

While NFL owners occasionally hired young, relatively inexperienced coaches to lead their teams, those hired had always been white. The League's head coaches of color tended to have long resumes and at least a few gray hairs, and Tomlin had neither. Indeed, while with Minnesota the previous year, Tomlin, born in 1972, was younger than two of his players and had played alongside one in college. Despite his youth, Tomlin commanded respect with the Vikings and had performed well, just as he had in his previous coaching stints. Still, particularly considering the Steelers' two internal candidates, Tomlin seemed a long shot at best.

Rooney, though, had fully internalized the philosophy and spirit in which the diverse candidate slate concept was rooted, and he had injected it into his organization's lifeblood. It did not matter that Rooney knew Grimm and Whisenhunt personally or that the press had portrayed his search as a two-person race. Rooney would not move forward without carefully and honestly considering all options, which meant meaningfully interviewing each candidate. He interviewed Rivera first, then Grimm, then Whisenhunt, all of whom performed admirably.

Finally he interviewed Tomlin, and he immediately learned what those closest to the young coach well knew: Tomlin was a fifty-year-old statesman in the body of a thirty-four-year-old football coach. His presence was overwhelming, engulfing the room. Straight-backed and square-shouldered, with a sincere smile and a firm handshake, Tomlin inspired confidence without saying a word. Tomlin did not have the experience his competitors boasted, and he had much to learn, but his inexperience did not impact his confidence as he outlined his plan for the Steelers' future. Tomlin's vision and enthusiasm intrigued Rooney, and after a few days of reflection and consultation with close confidants, Rooney hired Tomlin.

From the start, Tomlin imposed a no-nonsense culture in Pittsburgh. He demanded that every one of his players, even the stars, could and must improve, and he ran a notoriously rigorous training camp to ensure that it happened. Some of his players complained that the camp was, as one journalist phrased it, "intentionally savage." Others simply doubted the efficacy of Tomlin's methods. As Tomlin's first season progressed, however, his players increasingly bought in to his vision, and although the Steelers did not win a playoff game that year, Tomlin had constructed a solid foundation. In his second year, having built on that foundation, Tomlin delivered Rooney the ultimate thank-you: the Steelers' sixth Super Bowl victory.

The NFL's culture of equal opportunity, which had steadily burgeoned since 2002 and which Dan Rooney championed and ultimately embodied, afforded Mike Tomlin an interview he likely would not have secured otherwise. With the interview he got the job, and with the job he reached the mountaintop, becoming the third African American head coach in three years to lead his team to the Super Bowl and earning NFL Coach of the Year honors along the way.

According to most estimates, Tomlin's accomplishments set a high-water mark for the NFL's diversity efforts, but enthusiasm about those efforts would soon wane. By the end of the following head coach hiring cycle, many who had for years celebrated the League's equal opportunity commitment had grown disillusioned. Although the Buffalo Bills, in searching for a new head coach after a disappointing season, indisputably discharged their duties under the rule, the two other clubs in the head coach market, the Washington Redskins and Seattle Seahawks, sparked substantial controversy with their interviewing processes. The two searches were quite different, but critics believed they shared a common characteristic: they both flouted the Rooney Rule.

In the Redskins' case, owner Dan Snyder interviewed a candidate of color, the team's defensive backs coach, Jerry Gray, but he did so well before he fired his then-head coach Jim Zorn, and speculation reigned as to whether Snyder viewed Gray as a genuine candidate or as an employee he could manipulate into sitting for an ostensibly Rooney Rule–satisfying interview. The Seahawks handled their search differently. They did not interview a candidate of color before firing head coach Jim Mora Jr., but as soon as they fired him, they expressed intense interest in replacing him with Pete Carroll, the University of Southern California's head football coach. Amid media reports of an agreement in principle having been reached with Carroll, the Seahawks interviewed the Minnesota Vikings' African American defensive coordinator Leslie Frazier, then a few days later offered Carroll the job.

The FPA leadership, having spoken with Gray and Frazier as well as with the Redskins' and Seahawks' decision makers, concluded that both interviews, while perhaps suboptimal in form, were substantively meaningful and therefore satisfied both the letter and the spirit of the Rooney Rule. Still, many Rooney Rule supporters were unconvinced and called on the League to penalize both teams. Commissioner Goodell, however, insisted no penalty was warranted, disgruntling large segments of a community that had for the previous several years steadfastly supported the League's diversity efforts.

Fans who viewed the rule as unfair affirmative action, meanwhile, were up in arms for different reasons. Several months earlier, the NFL, pleased about the Rooney Rule's impact in the head coaching ranks, expanded the rule to cover a team's search for a general manager (or, in the case of the few teams that did not use the general manager title, the front office executive responsible for the team's football operations). Even many fans who had grudgingly accepted and in some cases supported the rule began to question both its expansion and its continued necessity. They noted that Jim Caldwell, who had replaced Tony Dungy in Indianapolis after the 2008 season, became in February 2010 the fourth African American in four years to lead his team to the Super Bowl. Moreover, they pointed out, the Arizona Cardinals, who lost to Tomlin's Steelers in the 2009 Super Bowl, and the New York Giants, who won the 2008 Super Bowl, both had African American general managers.

Indeed, some such fans pulled the Supreme Court's *Grutter v. Bollinger* affirmative action decision into the argument, noting that Justice Sandra Day O'Connor, who authored the majority opinion in that case, had suggested that the University of Michigan's plus-factor admissions policy, while reasonable at the time of the decision, might eventually grow unnecessary. Although O'Connor's time horizon in the *Grutter* case was twenty-five years, these fans wanted the Rooney Rule abandoned much sooner, and they expressed their displeasure.

The Rooney Rule and the manner in which the NFL was administering it were under attack from supporters and opponents alike. And although the League's precise path forward was unclear, Commissioner Goodell expressed no interest in scrapping the rule or otherwise pulling back on the League's diversity efforts. While the head coaches and general managers of color had generally been quite successful, their proportion of all NFL head coaches and general managers remained quite low (among the League's thirty-two teams, there were only six and five, respectively) and continued to lag far behind the proportion of the League's players of color.

How best to catalyze further change—whether through refining the Rooney Rule, as some of the rule's supporters were demanding, or through exploring other equity-inducing initiatives—was debatable, but there was no debating the track record the League had established over the course of the previous eight years. It had moved from having virtually no head coaching or front office diversity to being an industry leader in equal employment opportunity matters, and its efforts had begun to influence workplace diversity debates in other contexts. For better or for worse, depending on the perspective, the League had become a major player in the racial politics of the new millennium.

NOTES

Introduction

1 **as much a story as the game itself**: As a secondary matter, the event was notable because no two opposing Super Bowl coaches had previously posed together with the Super Bowl trophy. Author's interview with John Wooten.

2 **African American head coaches numbered a mere six**: Those six were Frederick Douglass "Fritz" Pollard, Art Shell, Dennis Green, Ray Rhodes, Tony Dungy, and Herman Edwards.

"Red Summer": The summer of 1919, dubbed "Red Summer" due to the widespread, bloody racial riots that characterized it, marked a low point in post-Reconstruction race relations. The riots began when white Americans who resented the sight of uniformed African American servicemen returning from World War I began attacking the soldiers, and the violence endured for months. For a thorough treatment of Red Summer, see Robert Whitaker, *On the Laps of Gods: The Red Summer of 1919 and the Struggle for Justice that Remade a Nation* (New York: Crown Publishers, 2008).

banning African Americans from its ranks altogether: Although some team owners would later deny actively expurgating African Americans from the NFL, it is generally recognized that the owners did, in fact, intentionally homogenize. Alexander Wolff, "The NFL's Jackie Robinson," *Sports Illustrated*, October 12, 2009, 63.

2 **following desegregation in 1946**: The Los Angeles Rams were the first
NFL team to desegregate. The team's decision in that regard, however, was
not a bold repudiation of segregation. It was, rather, a necessary consequence of the team's move from Cleveland to Los Angeles. Under pressure
from a powerful and persuasive African American journalist with the *Los
Angeles Tribune*, the commissioners of the Los Angeles Coliseum, in which
the team would play, insisted as part of the stadium agreement that the
Rams desegregate, which they did. Wolff, "The NFL's Jackie Robinson,"
66–68. Former UCLA football players Kenny Washington and Woody
Strode joined the Rams as the team's and League's only African American
players. African Americans Bill Willis and Marion Motley joined the
Cleveland Browns the same year, but the Browns, at that time, played in
the All-American Football Conference rather than the NFL. Ibid., 70.
   Despite the NFL's 1946 desegregation, "[w]hen Jackie Robinson integrated Major League Baseball in 1947, that event was hailed as the biggest
civil rights success since the Civil War." Kenneth Shropshire, *In Black and
White: Race and Sports in America* (New York: New York University Press,
1996), 19. Perhaps in part because professional baseball was at the time far
more popular in America than professional football (see Arthur Ashe Jr.,
A Hard Road to Glory: A History of the African-American Athlete Since 1946
[New York: Amistad Press, 1988], 128), Jackie Robinson's MLB debut was
then, and continues to be, viewed as the more significant milestone.
   (and, in the case of Major League Baseball, Latino) players: Well before
MLB's 1947 desegregation, light-skinned Latinos dotted major league rosters. Notably, even though they were permitted to play in the major
leagues before dark-skinned Latinos and African Americans, light-skinned
Latinos often suffered discriminatorily low pay and were degradingly ste-
reotyped. See Timothy Davis, "Racism in Athletics: Subtle Yet Persistent,"
21 *University of Arkansas Little Rock Law Review* 881, 890–91 (1999).
   The NBA featured its first head coach of color in 1966: In 1966, in addition to leading the Boston Celtics as its star center, Bill Russell accepted
the team's head coaching position. Ashe, *A Hard Road to Glory*, 57.
   Major League Baseball saw its first manager of color in 1975: On May 8,
1973, the Chicago Cubs' manager, Whitey Lockman, was ejected from a
game, and with no coaches available in the dugout to assume Lockman's
duties, one of the team's African American players, Ernie Banks, managed
the game's final two innings. Glenn Stout, *The Cubs: The Complete Story of
Chicago Cubs Baseball* (New York: Houghton Mifflin, 2007), 297–99. Dis-
counting that historical quirk, born as it was of happenstance rather than
intention, Frank Robinson is recognized as becoming MLB's first manger
of color in 1975 with the Cleveland Indians. Ashe, *A Hard Road to Glory*, 23.

3 **60 percent of the NFL's players were of color**: Michael Oriard, *Brand
NFL: Making and Selling America's Favorite Sport* (Chapel Hill: University
of North Carolina Press, 2007), 218.

3 **all thirty-two NFL head coaches were white**: Aside from Pollard, the NFL had, in its history, featured two other head coaches of color, both of whom were Latino. Tom Fears, born in Guadalajara, Mexico, to an American father and a Mexican mother, coached the New Orleans Saints from 1967 to 1970, and Tom Flores, also Mexican American, coached the Oakland Raiders from 1979 to 1987, winning two Super Bowl Championships along the way. Himilce Novas, *Everything You Need to Know About Latino History* (New York: Penguin, 2007), 368.

4 **the NFL's generally conservative culture**: The League has long exuded a subtle yet distinctively conservative air, which, as the Center for Responsive Politics reveals, is reflected in NFL community members' campaign donations. Although the study dates only to 1989, it concludes, "NFL owners, team officials, players, and coaches have overwhelmingly favored Republicans with their political contributions." Andy Barr, "NFL Kicks In Big for GOP," *Politico*, September 17, 2009, www.politico.com/news/stories/0909/27299.html. The trend may be changing, however. In 2008, the NFL created a political action committee called the Gridiron PAC, which in its short existence has donated more money to Democratic political candidates than Republican political candidates. Dave Levinthal, "Politicians Score Significant Cash from NFL Owners, Coaches, and Players," *Capital Eye Blog*, September 17, 2009, www.opensecrets.org/news/2009/09/politicians-score-significant.html.

Chapter 1: Baltimore Love

9 **"We were rooting for you today"**: Michael Smith, "It's Character, Not Color, That Separates Smith, Dungy," ESPN.com, January 24, 2007, http://sports.espn.go.com.nfl/playoffs06/columns/story?   columnist=smith_michael&id=2740318.

10 **Irsay skipped town with his team**: Clark Judge, "Quarter-Century Later, Irsay the Younger Helps Heal Wounds," CBSSports.com, March 27, 2009, www.cbssports.com/nfl/story/11557831. Baltimore did ultimately launch condemnation proceedings, and for a year Irsay and the city battled in court over rights to the team. Charles C. Euchner, *Playing the Field: Why Sports Teams Move and Cities Fight to Keep Them* (Baltimore: Johns Hopkins University Press, 1994), 111.

11 **famous for once pelting Santa Claus with snowballs**: Although authors Glen Macnow and Anthony L. Gargano, in their book *The Great Philadelphia Fan Book*, acknowledge the incident, they argue that fans' displeasure with the then-floundering Eagles organization, rather than evil intent, motivated the snowball attack. Glen Macnow and Anthony L. Gargano, *The Great Philadelphia Fan Book* (Moorestown, NJ: Middle Atlantic Press, 2003), 36.
"vicious": Tony Dungy, *Quiet Strength* (Carol Stream, IL: Tyndale House, 2007), 278.

11 **"we want you to win and get to the Super Bowl"**: Smith, "It's Character, Not Color, That Separates Smith, Dungy."

14 **Smith might never have ascended to a head coaching position at all**: Just days before the Bears' Super Bowl appearance, Smith admitted as much: "I would like to think owners would hire the best coach but I'm here because of the Rooney Rule." Clifton Brown, "Bears Hope Takeaways Lead Them to a Title," *New York Times*, January 30, 2007, D2.

Chapter 2: An Idea's Origin

15 **than most people knew or were willing to admit**: For more on what some describe as this "new racism," see Eduardo Bonilla-Silva, *Racism Without Racists: Color-Blind Racism and the Persistence of Racial Inequality in the United States* (New York: Rowman and Littlefield, 2006).

"second-generation" discrimination: Author's interview with Cyrus Mehri.

16 **Civil Rights Act of 1964**: 42 U.S.C. § 1971 et seq.

Voting Rights Act of 1965: 42 U.S.C. § 1973 et seq.

Fair Housing Act of 1968: 42 U.S.C. § 3601 et seq.

Title VII, which prohibits employers from terminating: Title VII's precise language on this score is: "It shall be an unlawful employment practice for an employer . . . to fail or refuse to hire or to discharge any individual, or otherwise to discriminate against any individual with respect to his compensation, terms, conditions, or privileges of employment, because of such individual's race, color, religion, sex, or national origin. . . ." 42 U.S.C. 2000e-2(a)(1).

18 **"Dungy Out"**: "Dungy Out, Parcells May Be In," *Washington Post*, January 15, 2002, D8.

death of one of the team's best offensive linemen: On the second day of the Vikings' 2001 training camp, All-Pro offensive lineman Korey Stringer collapsed in the searing heat, ultimately dying of heatstroke. His wife, Kelci, subsequently sued the NFL for wrongful death, arguing the League did not sufficiently protect players from heat-related ailments. In January 2009, as part of an agreement settling the case, the NFL agreed to support Kelci's efforts to establish a "heat illness prevention program." "Stringer's Widow Settles Lawsuit with NFL," *New York Times*, January 27, 2009, B15.

among NFL head coaches and called for change: See, e.g., Mike Freeman, "On Pro Football: Path to the Top Job Is Biased," *New York Times*, February 6, 2000, sec. 8, 2; Norman Chad, "NFL Coaching Material Could Be Cut from More Colorful Cloth," *Washington Post*, September 9, 1997, D8.

19 **"coached the Buccaneers for four losing seasons before being fired"**: Johnnie L. Cochran Jr. and Cyrus Mehri, *Black Coaches in the National Football League: Superior Performance, Inferior Opportunities* (self-published, September 30, 2002), 12.

20 **sixteen matches on the road**: Peter King, "Green Bay Packers: New Coach and Old Friend Ray Rhodes Is Singing a One-Big-Happy-Family Tune as the Pack Makes One More Run, but Father Time Is Creeping Up," *Sports Illustrated*, August 30, 1999, 185–86.

22 **rampant organization-wide racial discrimination**: Texaco's defense collapsed when Mehri and his co-counsel stumbled upon surreptitiously recorded audio tapes of Texaco executives' conversations. The recordings revealed the executives "destroying or altering documents that had been sought in the case" and, while doing so, using such racially offensive language that the whole scene "sounded like a Ku Klux Klan rally." Bari-Ellen Roberts and Jack E. White, *Roberts v. Texaco: A True Story of Race and Corporate America* (New York: Avon, 1998), 255.

23 **massive racially driven disparities**: Constance Hays, in *The Real Thing: Truth and Power at the Coca-Cola Company*, details the disparities: "The database showed that blacks were clustered disproportionately in the lowest-paying jobs and further marginalized by being confined to certain departments and roles. They were almost never promoted to top management positions. . . . The median salary for blacks at Coke in 1998 was $36,296, according to the database, while the median salary for whites was nearly twice that, at $65,531." Constance L. Hays, *The Real Thing: Truth and Power at the Coca-Cola Company*, (New York: Random House, 2004), 214.

24 **"You can't win"**: Author's interview with Cyrus Mehri.

representing the company as defense counsel: Hays, *The Real Thing*, 261, 340.

contacted Mehri and Bondurant Mixson and requested to be co-counsel: Author's interview with Cyrus Mehri.

25 **not sure how his name had materialized on the complaint**: Ibid.

Thirteenth Amendment's promise that slavery was no more: The Thirteenth Amendment to the United States Constitution reads, in relevant part, as follows: "Neither slavery nor involuntary servitude, except as a punishment for crime whereof the party shall have been duly convicted, shall exist within the United States, or any place subject to their jurisdiction." U.S. CONSTITUTION, Amend. XIII, § 1.

the institution of sharecropping: For a fascinating firsthand account of a sharecropper's life—a life, perhaps, similar to those of Alonzo and Hannah Cochran—see Theodore Rosengarten, *All God's Dangers: The Life of Nate Shaw* (Chicago: University of Chicago Press, 1974).

26 **"in Louisiana, in 1935, mistakes were of no consequence"**: Johnnie L. Cochran Jr., *Journey to Justice* (New York: Ballantine, 1996), 16.

"make an impression wherever you go, on every level": Ibid., 15.

27 **educational philosophy to be fatally flawed**: The Court's decision, delivered by Chief Justice Earl Warren, was unanimous. *Brown v. Board of Education of Topeka, Kansas*, 347 U.S. 483 (1954).

"inherently *unequal*": Ibid., 495 (emphasis added).

28 **"race card"**: DeWayne Wickham, "Spare Cochran Legacy of 'Race Card' Label," *USA Today*, April 5, 2005, 15A.

"responded to the cards he was dealt": Ibid.

29 **his affiliation with the Black Panther Party**: For a detailed account of Pratt's affiliation with the Black Panther Party, Pratt's murder trial, and Cochran's advocacy on Pratt's behalf, see Jack Olsen, *Last Man Standing: The Tragedy and Triumph of Geronimo Pratt* (New York: Doubleday, 2000).

Chapter 3: Superior Performance, Inferior Opportunities

33 **"to get a job as a head coach in the NFL"**: Cochran and Mehri, *Black Coaches in the National Football League*, Exhibit B, 3.

averaging 2.7 more wins over the sixteen-game regular season: Ibid.

averaging 1.3 more wins: Ibid., 4.

white coaches led their teams to eight wins per season: Ibid., 2.

34 **fewer than 10 percent of teams winning eight games did the same**: Ibid.

after they were fired, the teams got worse: The African American coaches averaged 9.1 wins per season, whereas their preceding white coaches averaged 7.4 wins per season and their succeeding white coaches averaged 8.9 wins per season. Ibid., 5.

36 **"is declared to be illegal"**: 15 U.S.C. § 1.

the NFL launched the single-entity defense: "The NFL," the court explained in synopsizing the league's argument, "contends the league structure is in essence a singly entity, akin to a partnership or joint venture, precluding application of Sherman Act section 1 which prevents only contracts, combinations or conspiracies in restraint of trade." *Los Angeles Memorial Coliseum Commission v. National Football League*, 726 F.2d 1381, 1387 (9th Cir. 1984). Over the years, in subsequent antitrust cases, the NFL has made the same single-entity argument, and most recently in *American Needle Inc. v. National Football League* the United States Court of Appeals for the Seventh Circuit accepted it. See *American Needle, Inc. v. National Football League*, 538 F.3d 736 (7th Cir. 2008). The United States Supreme Court, however, reversed in a unanimous decision. See *American Needle, Inc. v. National Football League*, 130 S.Ct. 2201 (2010).

37 **"We don't get one"**: Gordon Edes, "Harper Finally at Home," *Boston Globe*, February 1, 2006, D2.

38 **"we don't allow any niggers in here"**: Howard Bryant, *Shut Out: A Story of Race and Baseball in Boston* (New York: Routledge, 2002), 147.

"It was like I had dropped a bomb or something": Michael Madden, "Harper: Sox Are Racist," *Boston Globe*, January 31, 1986, 39.

39 **United States Equal Employment Opportunity Commission (EEOC)**: Congress, in enacting Title VII of the Civil Rights Act of 1964, established the EEOC "to prevent any person from engaging in any unlawful

employment practice as set forth" in Title VII. 42 U.S.C. § 2000e-5(a). Under EEOC procedures, a complaining party must, prior to filing suit under Title VII, file a formal discriminatory charge with the EEOC. Further, the complaining party must do so within 300 days of the alleged discriminatory act or, if the state within which the alleged discriminatory act occurred has no EEOC analog, within 180 days of the alleged discriminatory act. If after assessing the charge, the EEOC opts against taking action, the complaining party has 90 days within which to file suit in federal court. 42 U.S.C. § 2000e-5(e)(1).

39 **"would have been terminated"**: Michael Madden, "Harper Charges Against Sox Upheld," *Boston Globe*, July 2, 1986, 67.

"perpetuated a working environment hostile to minorities": Ibid.

a low six-figure settlement: The precise terms of the settlement were not publicly disclosed, but the *Boston Globe*'s Gordon Edes reports Harper received "a few thousand dollars." Edes, "Harper Finally at Home," D2.

40 **criminally prosecuted Johnson and forced him out of the country**: For more on the persecution and prosecution of Jack Johnson, see Geoffrey Ward, *Unforgivable Blackness: The Rise and Fall of Jack Johnson* (New York: Alfred A. Knopf), 296–349.

black-gloved fists: Although media reports described the runners' protest as a hate-infused black-power salute, it was not. Both Smith and Carlos were members of the Olympic Project for Human Rights, whose founder, San Jose State University sociologist Harry Edwards, aimed to expose racial inequality in the sports industry and in America more generally. Edwards initially called upon American athletes to boycott the 1968 Olympic Games, but the boycott did not materialize, leaving each athlete who believed in the project's mission to forward it in his or her own way. Smith and Carlos did so through their protest, which—it bears noting, considering the media reports—the race's second-place winner, a white Australian, fully supported. Allen Barra, "Fists Raised, but Not in Anger," *New York Times*, August 8, 2008, A19.

they endured decades of abuse: Analogized to Nazis in the press, Smith and Carlos each received death threats and encountered difficulty finding employment. A decade after the Mexico City Olympics, Carlos's wife committed suicide, and he attributed the tragedy in part to the hostility the couple suffered in the years following the protest. Megan Falater, "Tommie Smith and John Carlos," in Matthew C. Whitaker, ed., *African American Icons of Sport: Triumph, Courage, and Excellence* (Westport, CT: Greenwood, 2008), 250–52.

racial discrimination in the professional sports industry: Craig Hodges, a former Chicago Bulls basketball player, is the notable exception. In 1996, Hodges sued the NBA, alleging the league's teams conspired to exclude him because of his race and because "his political activities were not welcomed by the NBA." See *Hodges v. National Basketball Association*, 1998 WL 26193, *1 (N.D. Ill. 1998). Five years earlier, when the Bulls visited the White House after winning the 1991 NBA Championship, Hodges appeared in "traditional African vestments and presented a letter to President Bush calling for an end to injustice toward the African American community." Ibid. The Bulls expressed displeasure with Hodges and refused to re-sign him after his contract lapsed, and in spite of Hodges' basketball playing talent, no other NBA team ever gave him a tryout. Ibid. The United States District Court for the Northern District of Illinois did not reach the merits of Hodges' case, dismissing it as untimely. Ibid., 7.

43 **"best values of our society"**: Cochran and Mehri, *Black Coaches in the National Football League*, 1.

44 **"don't mention litigation"**: Author's interview with Cyrus Mehri.

45 **the match's sponsors had withdrawn their financial support**: Despite protests, new financial backing emerged, the Nashville, Tennessee–based Ku Klux Klan chapter promised to protect spectators from civil rights demonstrators, and the matches ultimately took place. Demonstrators, however, outnumbered spectators by a three-to-one margin and the event was financially unsuccessful. Richard Lapchick, *Smashing Barriers: Race and Sport in the New Millennium* (New York: Madison Books, 2001), 60–86.

"You know you have no business in South Africa": Ibid., 7.

were carved into his naked stomach: Ibid., 10.

The attack terrified Lapchick: The attack's aftermath further traumatized Lapchick, as some factions of the Norfolk, Virginia, police department and some examining physicians hypothesized that he "staged the attack." Lapchick ultimately took, and passed, a polygraph test to prove his veracity. Ibid., 37–56.

the "conscience of sport": Richard Lapchick, *New Game Plan for College Sport* (Westport, CT: Greenwood, 2002), 307; Jean Patterson, "Punches Thrown, Hits Taken," *Orlando Sentinel*, June 5, 2005, F1. In 1997, the Aetna Foundation honored Lapchick for his life's work with the prestigious Arthur Ashe Voice of Conscience Award. Scott Powers, "UCF Hires Ethics Crusader to Launch Sports Program," *Orlando Sentinel*, August 24, 2001, A1.

46 **"No. I won't mention litigation"**: Author's interview with Cyrus Mehri.

47 **"we will litigate"**: Ibid.

his recently released memoir, *A Lawyer's Life*: Johnnie L. Cochran Jr., *A Lawyer's Life* (New York: St. Martin's, 2002).

48 **"You can mark our words on that"**: HBO's *Real Sports with Bryant Gumbel* (2002).

49 **"Don't let it stop you"**: Author's interview with Cyrus Mehri.

Chapter 4: Enter the Godfather

54 **"If they don't make that integration decision, I'm dead"**: Author's interview with John Wooten.

56 **"I just don't understand what you're doing, Woots"**: Ibid.

57 **"will get a chance to play pro football"**: Richard Goldstein, "Tank Younger, 73, First Star From Black College to Play in N.F.L., Dies," *New York Times*, September 19, 2001, C15.

59 **San Francisco 49ers head coach Bill Walsh**: Walsh was famously cerebral, and his legendary innovations remained NFL fixtures long after his retirement from NFL head coaching in 1989. "Bill Walsh, Innovator of West Coast Offense, Dies at 75," *New York Times*, July 31, 2007, B9. Most notably, he pioneered the "West Coast offense," which features a barrage of short passes designed to control the ball and disrupt any defensive scheme. Ibid. **quality control assistants**: NFL quality control assistants are generally marginally paid junior members of coaching staffs and are usually not responsible for coaching any particular position. Instead, they help the team in a variety of other capacities, such as data entry, game film analysis, and assisting more senior coaches during practice drills. Greg Bishop, "For Little Glory, NFL Quality-Control Coaches Learn It All," *New York Times*, September 27, 2009, SP1.

60 **"screaming and hollering" sessions**: Author's interview with John Wooten.

Chapter 5: The Rooney Rule

63 **"They didn't need me there"**: Author's interview with Jeffrey Pash.

65 **"radical liberal"**: Frank Lynn, "Charles E. Goodell, Former Senator, Is Dead at 60," *New York Times*, January 22, 1987, B20.

71 **"headline-grabbing, self-serving outsiders"**: Author's interview with Harold Henderson.

72 **Rooney was a giant**: On March 17, 2009, President Obama, recognizing what those in the NFL long had, nominated Rooney to be U.S. ambassador to Ireland. Judy Battista, "Steelers' Rooney Is Named Ambassador to Ireland," *New York Times*, March 18, 2009, B11.

76 **"in this country attached to me"**: Kellen Winslow, foreword, in Shropshire, *In Black and White*, xi.

77 **"Why are we talking with you, then?"**: Author's interview with Kellen Winslow; author's interview with Tom Williamson.
"that you would talk about that stuff": Author's interview with Kellen Winslow; author's interview with Tom Williamson.
"published a report to pillory the League": Author's interview with Tom Williamson.

78 **"There's nothing new about that"**: Ibid.

79 **"what better idea do you have?":** Ibid.
80 **"An open letter to Paul Tagliabue":** Luke Smith, "An open letter to Paul Tagliabue," *Michigan Daily*, October 3, 2002, 4A.
"white wide receivers are being held to higher standards": Ibid.
81 **using such "plus factors" in admitting students:** *Grutter v. Bollinger*, 288 F.3d 732, 748 (6th Cir. 2001).
upheld the policy against legal challenge: Ibid., 752.
United Steelworkers v. Weber: 443 U.S. 193 (1979).
"the historical context from which the Act arose": *United Steelworkers v. Weber*, 443 U.S. 193, 201 (1979).
to protect the employment opportunities of people of color: Ibid., 203; Michael L. Foreman, Kristin M. Dadey, and Audrey J. Wiggins, "The Continuing Relevance of Race-Conscious Remedies and Programs in Integrating the Nation's Workforce," 22 *Hofstra Labor and Employment Law Journal* 81, 97 (2004); Emmanuel O. Iheukwumere and Phillip C. Aka, "Title VII, Affirmative Action, and the March Toward Color-Blind Jurisprudence," 11 *Temple Political and Civil Rights Law Review* 1, 23 (2001).
"conspicuous" or "manifest" "racial imbalance": Charles A. Sullivan, "Circling Back to the Obvious: The Convergence of Traditional and Reverse Discrimination in Title VII Proof," 46 *William and Mary Law Review* 1031, 1048 (2004). Precisely what constitutes a conspicuous or manifest imbalance is unclear. See Cynthia L. Estlund, "Putting *Grutter* to Work: Diversity, Integration, and Affirmative Action in the Workplace," 26 *Berkeley Journal of Employment and Labor Law* 1, 12 (2005); Rebecca Hanner White, "Affirmative Action in the Workplace: The Significance of *Grutter*?" 92 *Kentucky Law Journal* 263, 267 (2003–2004).
"unduly trammel the interests of majority group members": Sullivan, "Circling Back to the Obvious," 1051; Robert Belton, "Brown as a Work in Progress: Still Seeking Consensus After All These Years," 34 *Stetson Law Review* 487, 495 (2005).
Johnson v. Transportation Agency: 480 U.S. 616, 627 (1987).
"or was a permanent, rather than a temporary, plan": N. Jeremi Duru, "Fielding a Team for the Fans: The Societal Consequences and Title VII Implications of Race-Considered Roster Construction in Professional Sport," 84 *Washington University Law Review* 375, 411 (2006) quoting Sullivan, "Circling Back to the Obvious," 1051.
82 ***Richmond v. J. A. Croson Co.:*** 488 U.S. 469 (1989).
Adarand Constructors, Inc. v. Pena: 515 U.S. 200 (1995).
University of Michigan's "plus factors" affirmative action plan: *Grutter v. Bollinger*, 539 U.S. 306 (2003).
not only in the classroom but in the workplace: Ibid., 330; Foreman, Dadey and Wiggins, "Continuing Relevance of Race-Conscious Remedies and Programs," 102.

83 **attempted to limit African Americans' numbers on their rosters**: For a thorough exploration of such "race-considered roster construction" and its consequences, see Duru, "Fielding a Team for the Fans."

"sharp contrast with the composition of the league": Duru, "Fielding a Team for the Fans," 395–96. The Celtics' consistent racial disproportionality inspired a league-wide running joke: "white plus height equals a job with the Boston Celtics." Bryant, *Shut Out*, 144.

intentionally considered race in crafting the team's roster: See Gregory Witcher and Jonathan Kaufman, "Blacks Split on Backing Celtics," *Boston Globe*, June 4, 1987, 1.

"the back end of their roster with token whites": Harvey Araton and Filip Bondy, *The Selling of the Green: The Financial Rise and Moral Decline of the Boston Celtics* (New York: HarperCollins, 1992), 125.

84 **"the Celtics [were] synonymous with whiteness"**: Michael Wilbon, "A Perceptible Change," *Washington Post*, June 5, 2008, E1. In light of this organizational identity, Wilbon writes, the Celtics were inescapably conspicuous as they appeared in the 2008 NBA Championship with an almost exclusively African American team. Ibid.

"but I need white people. It's in me": Araton and Bondy, *The Selling of the Green*, 181.

outstripped the percentage of white players in NBA at large: Duru, "Fielding a Team for the Fans," 400.

demanded a substantial representation of white players: See, e.g., James V. Koch and C. Warren Vander Hill, "Is There Discrimination in the 'Black Man's Game'?" 6 *Social Science Quarterly* 83 (1988); Jerome Karabel and David Karen, "Color on the Court," *In These Times*, February 10–16, 1982, 23–24; Daniel R. Vining and James F. Kerrigan, "An Application of the Lexis Ratio to the Detection of Racial Quotas in Professional Sports: A Note," 22 *American Economist* 71 (1978); Joseph M. Markmann, "A Note on Discrimination by Race in Professional Basketball," 20 *American Economist* 65 (1976).

Other studies, focusing primarily on what their authors' concluded to be a reduced or eliminated racial salary gap in the NBA, asserted the cessation of notable customer discrimination in that league. See, e.g., Frank A. Scott, James E. Long, and Ken Somppi, "Salary vs. Marginal Revenue Product Under Monopsony and Competition—The Case of Professional Basketball," 13 *Atlantic Economic Journal* 50 (1985); Charles E. Rockwood and Ephraim Asher, "Racial Discrimination in Professional Basketball Revisited," 20 *American Economist* 59 (1976).

"have a taste for seeing white players": Eleanor Brown, Diane Keenan, and Richard Spiro, "Wage and Nonwage Discrimination in Professional Basketball: Do Fans Affect It?" 50 *American Journal of Economics and Sociology* 333, 343 (1991).

85　**47.4 percent were African American and 52.6 percent were white**: Araton and Bondy, *The Selling of the Green*, 124.

continued existence of racial considerations in roster construction: See, e.g., Paul T. Schollaert and Donald H. Smith, "Team Racial Composition and Sports Attendance," 28 *Sociological Quarterly* 71 (1987).

"[NBA] teams [were still] responding to customer discrimination": Richard Burdekin, Richard Hossfeld, and Janet Smith, "Are NBA Fans Becoming Indifferent to Race? Evidence from the 1990s," 6 *Journal of Sports Economics* 144, 147–48 (2002). Burdekin, Hossfeld, and Smith note that although their study does not suggest that the NBA as a whole erects racially discriminatory barriers to entry, "there remains a correlation between a team's racial composition and the racial composition of the city in which the team is based." Ibid., 155.

"characterized by customer discrimination": Ilyana M. Kuziemko and Geoffrey C. Rapp, "Customer Racial Discrimination in Major League Baseball: Is There No Hope for Equal Pay?," 7 *Texas Hispanic Journal of Law and Policy* 119, 142 (2001). It bears noting that scholars are not united on this score. For instance, economists Craig A. Depken II and Jon M. Ford, examining fan selection of MLB All-Star Game participants between the years 1990 and 2000, concluded, in that context, that there did not appear to exist customer-based discrimination against players of color. See Craig A. Depken II and Jon M. Ford, "Customer-Based Discrimination Against Major League Baseball Players: Additional Evidence from All-Star Ballots," 35 *Journal of Socio-Economics* 1061 (2006).

both of whom had short stints: The first was Willie Thrower, who in 1953 entered just two games as a backup quarterback with the Chicago Bears, completed three of eight pass attempts, and never played in the League again. Frank Litsky, "Willie Thrower, 71, First Black Quarterback," *New York Times*, February 23, 2002, B8. The second was Marlin Briscoe, who played quarterback for the Denver Broncos (then of the American Football League) in 1968 before being cut during the Broncos' 1969 training camp. Michael MacCambridge, *America's Game: The Epic Story of How Pro Football Captured a Nation* (New York: Random House, 2004), 248–50; Bill Rhoden, "Black Quarterbacks: One Foot In The Door," *Ebony Magazine*, November 1974, 167.

86　**when attempting to transition to the professional ranks**: This discriminatory tradition has endured. Indeed, two of the 2006 Super Bowl champion Pittsburgh Steelers' best wide receivers—Antwaan Randle-El and Hines Ward—played the quarterback position in college. While Ward played quarterback, running back, and wide receiver at the University of Georgia (see Tim Layden, "His Mother's Son," *Sports Illustrated*, October 13, 1997, 113–15), Randel-El was strictly a quarterback at Indiana University and was one of the nation's best, placing sixth in balloting for the Heisman Trophy, an annual award given to college football's best player. Andrew Bagnato, "Huskers' Crouch Proves Best Option; Nebraska QB Edges Grossman; Randle El 6th," *Chicago Tribune*, December 9, 2001, C1.

86 **had been selected in the draft's first round**: Lapchick, *Smashing Barriers*, 228.

African Americans constituting 65 percent of the League's players: Richard Lapchick, *2003 Racial and Gender Report Card*, 14, www.tidesport.org/RGRC/2003/2003%20RGRC.pdf.

they accounted for only 22 percent of the League's quarterbacks: Of the League's eighty-one quarterbacks at the time, eighteen were African American. Those eighteen follow, in alphabetical order: Tony Banks, Jeff Blake, Aaron Brooks, Henry Burris, Quincy Carter, Daunte Culpepper, Rohan Davey, David Gerrard, Jarious Jackson, Shaun King, Ray Lucas, Donovan McNabb, Steve McNair, Rodney Peete, Akili Smith, Kordell Stewart, Michael Vick, and Troy Woodbury.

"being held to higher standards": Smith, "An Open Letter to Paul Tagliabue," 4A.

The Rooney Rule was born: The rule, as enacted, provided an exception for teams contractually obligated to promote an assistant coach to the head coach position upon the head coach's departure. Danny O'Neil, "Seahawks Passing the Torch: Secondary Coach Mora Will Take Over for Holmgren After 2008 season," *Seattle Times*, February 7, 2008, D2.

Chapter 6: The Coaching Carousel

88 **"Cyrus, you came out of nowhere and changed the NFL"**: Author's interview with Cyrus Mehri.

89 **"500 coaches who could have won the Super Bowl"**: Michael Silver, "Special . . . Delivery: The Steelers Handed the Cowboys Two Ugly Interceptions and a 27–17 Victory," *Sports Illustrated*, February 5, 1996, 35.

90 **be examined for toxic mold**: Chip Brown, "Seven Things to Ponder: Jerry Jones and the Cowboys Must Answer These Questions Before the Season Ends," *Dallas Morning News*, November 1, 2002, B1.

92 **"Julia Roberts in 'Runaway Bride'"**: Tony Kornheiser, "Parcells and Jones: Bill and Coo," *Washington Post*, January 2, 2003, D1.

"general talks about football and the NFL": Rich Cimini, "He Can Be America's Tuna: Parcells Admits Dallas Interest," *New York Daily News*, December 22, 2002, 46.

"discussed pro football, philosophy and the Cowboys": Ibid.

93 **"would have to be considered meaningless"**: Leonard Shapiro, "Many Titles, but Very Little Straight Talk from Parcells, Cowboys' Jones," *Washington Post*, December 25, 2002, D5.

94 **"whirlwind two-week courtship"**: Leonard Shapiro and Mark Maske, "After 3 Years at Pasture, Parcells Rides in to Dallas," *Washington Post*, January 3, 2003, D1.
"It looks like the old regime, not a new day": Leonard Shapiro, "Parcells Pursuit May Violate NFL Policy," *Washington Post*, December 30, 2002, D12.
"and they said, 'That's the guy I want'": Author's interview with Roger Goodell.

95 **"Let's see what happens, and then let's make an assessment"**: Author's interview with Jeffrey Pash.
"ruling anything out": Shapiro, "Parcells Pursuit May Violate NFL Policy," D12.

96 **"antiquated and doddering"**: Paul Daugherty, "Hire of Lewis Step in Right Direction for Bengals," *USA Today*, January 15, 2003, 5C.
"the Flintstones of the NFL," as one former Bengal put it: Ibid.
"This is the policy, and we will comply": Mark Curnutte, "Bengals Will Search Near, Far for Coach," *Cincinnati Enquirer*, December 31, 2002, D1.
"poster child": Mark Curnutte, "Positions of Authority Lily-White for Bengals," *Cincinnati Enquirer*, December 1, 2002, 3C.

97 **interviewed a person of color for any of those positions**: Ibid.
"lily-white": Ibid.

98 **Cincinnati police officers had killed fourteen African American men**: Dan Horn, "Prologue to Turmoil: 'A Very Tense Time,'" *Cincinnati Enquirer*, December 30, 2001, 2G.
A study of 141,000 traffic tickets: Doug Trapp, "Moving Violations: Racial Profiling by the Numbers," *City Beat*, March 8–14, 2001, 13.
lawsuit against the Cincinnati Police Department: Horn, "Prologue to Turmoil," 2G. An individual, Bomani Tyehimba, originally filed the action in 1999, but in 2001 he moved to amend his complaint to include class claims on behalf of African American Cincinnatans. *In re Cincinnati Policing*, 209 F.R.D 395, 397 (S.D. Ohio 2002).

99 **"He has, ah, about 14 warrants on him"**: NBC's *Dateline*, April 10, 2004.
what had happened that night in the Bronx: B. Keith Payne, "Prejudice and Perception: The Role of Automatic and Controlled Processes in Misperceiving a Weapon," 81 *Journal of Personality and Social Psychology* 181 (2001).

100 **"even ones we may not necessarily endorse or believe"**: Malcolm Gladwell, *Blink: The Power of Thinking Without Thinking* (New York: Little, Brown, 2005), 232.
"we know that wallets invariably look like guns": Ibid., 243.

103 **"would it have been one out of [six]? I don't think so"**: Don Banks, "Dungy Lashes Out: Lewis Omission Has Bucs Head Coach Questioning Process," CNNSI.com, February 1, 2001, http://sportsillustrated.cnn.com/inside_game/don_banks/news/2001/02/01/dungy_insider_banks/.

103 **"than hire a black head coach"**: Michael Wilbon, "What's a Should-Be Head Coach to Do?" *Washington Post*, December 10, 2002, D1.

106 **"how best to utilize our various talents"**: Buster Olney, "Seeking Power, 49ers' Coach Loses His Job," *New York Times*, January 16, 2003, D1.

Chapter 7: Millen, Mooch, and the Great Detroit Hiring Debate

107 **"The same reasons that I hired him still exist, and we move forward"**: Michael Rosenberg, "After Vote of Confidence, Lions Sack Mornhinweg," *Detroit Free Press*, January 28, 2003, 5D.

108 **"they knew it in Tokyo"**: Michael Rosenberg, "Minorities Left Behind in NFL Coaching Circles," *Detroit Free Press*, February 4, 2003, 1D.

109 **"process"**: Lynn Henning, "Millen Quick to Defend Hiring Process," *Detroit News*, February 6, 2003, 7E.

110 **"state of the NFL" news conference**: Leonard Shapiro, "Rules for OT May Change—Tagliabue Also Defends NFL's Minority Hiring Initiatives," *Washington Post*, January 25, 2003, D4.
"respect for them as individuals": Hank Gola, "No Cold Shoulder for NYC," *New York Daily News*, January 25, 2003, 50.

111 **"to see what occurred and where to proceed in the future"**: Leonard Shapiro, "Mariucci Hiring Draws Criticism—Officials: Minority Candidates Ignored," *Washington Post*, February 5, 2003, D4.

112 **he was deeply displeased**: Author's interview with Jeffrey Pash. Several days after the Lions hired Mariucci, Gene Upshaw spoke publicly about Rooney's private discontentment: "We were all satisfied with where [the Rooney Rule] was going until we saw the Detroit situation. Even Rooney, it takes a lot to get him upset. He felt it was a mockery of what everyone agreed to abide by." Judy Battista, "Lions' Cursory Glance Catches League's Eye," *New York Times*, February 9, 2003, sec. 8, 4.

113 **"never given a fair chance to interview"**: Henning, "Millen Quick to Defend Hiring Process," 7E.
Jesse Jackson had entered the Rooney Rule fray: "Jackson Calls for Inquiry of Lions," *Detroit Free Press*, February 8, 2003, 3B.
"a magnificence of spirit and an appalling crassness": Marshall Frady, *Jesse: The Life and Pilgrimage of Jesse Jackson* (New York: Random House, 1996), 27.

114 **"blacks could not be quarterbacks" at Illinois**: Kenneth Timmerman, *Shakedown: Exposing the Real Jesse Jackson* (Washington, DC: Regnery, 2002), 13.
Illini's starting quarterback that year, was African American: Ibid.
"a culture driven by white supremacists": André Douglas Pond Cummings, "'Lions and Tigers and Bears, Oh My' or 'Redskins and Braves and Indians, Oh Why': Ruminations on *McBride v. Utah State Tax Commission*,

Political Correctness, and the Reasonable Person," 36 *California Western Law Review* 11, 23n70 (1999).

114 **"Detroit Lions general manager and the Ford family"**: Steve Schrader, "City Council Takes Lions to Task over Hiring Process," *Detroit Free Press*, February 13, 2003, 2D.

115 **"this kind of issue in professional football"**: Michael Wilbon, "Hung Out to Dry on the Color Line," *Washington Post*, February 14, 2003, D1.

Chapter 8: Birth of an Alliance

120 **"You have to talk to them like football guys"**: Author's interview with John Wooten; author's interview with Cyrus Mehri.

121 **"Right now, all of your names are Paul"**: Author's interview with Kellen Winslow.

122 **"they may as well refer to you as Paul, à la Paul Tagliabue"**: Ibid.
"they won't know who you are until you organize": Ibid.
"an affinity group to represent your interests": Author's interview with Cyrus Mehri.

123 **"so that the base of candidates gets stronger and stronger"**: Ibid.

124 **"come down on this and people will lose jobs"**: Author's interview with Cyrus Mehri; author's interview with John Wooten.

125 **"If heads are going to roll, let it be my head"**: Author's interview with Cyrus Mehri; author's interview with John Wooten; author's interview with Terry Robiskie.
"we can make this work": Author's interview with Tony Dungy.

128 **"respond to it in an appropriate and proportionate way"**: Author's interview with Jeffrey Pash.
"best interests" of baseball: Major League Agreement, Art. I, Sec. 2(a) (1921).
The NFL was no exception: The NFL's Constitution and Bylaws read, in relevant part: "The Commissioner is authorized . . . to . . . take or adopt appropriate legal action or such other steps or procedures as he deems necessary and proper in the best interests of either the League or professional football, whenever any party or organization not a member of, employed by, or connected with the League or any member thereof is guilty of any conduct detrimental either to the League, its member clubs or employees, or to professional football." National Football League Constitution and Bylaws, Art. VIII, Sec. 6.
"conduct detrimental": Ibid.

129 **"embrace inclusive hiring practices going forward"**: Patrick K. Thornton, "The Increased Opportunity for Minorities in the National Football League Coaching Ranks: The Initial Success of the NFL's Rooney Rule," *Willamette Sports Law Journal*, 52 (2009), www.willamette.edu/wucl/journals/sportslaw/documents/Spring%202009%20-%204.pdf.

129 **"I think it's a shame and totally unwarranted"**: Sam Farmer, "Lion Officials Criticize $200,000 Fine on Millen," *Los Angeles Times*, July 29, 2003,
D3.

choosing to formally "disagree" with Tagliabue's decision: Mark Maske,
"Lions' Millen Is Fined $200,000—Minority Coaching Interviews at
Issue," *Washington Post*, July 26, 2003, D1.

Chapter 9: A Season of Dreams

132 **"we won't get a very good deal"**: Gary Myers, "Lewis Faces First-and-
Long," *Daily News*, March 30, 2003, 77.

"captain who knows we're on his burial site": Gerald Eskenazi, "Palmer
Faces Reality in Debut," *New York Times*, August 11, 2003, 5.

the Bengals paid the bonus anyway: Myers, "Lewis Faces First-and-
Long," 77.

"to the 21st century in less than three months": Ibid.

133 **"romantic notion"**: Eskenazi, "Palmer Faces Reality in Debut," 5.

134 **"he has to change the culture of a losing team"**: Ibid.

he was, in his own words, excited: Ibid.

since the stadium opened three years earlier: "Palmer, Bengals Earn Positive Reviews," *Washington Post*, August 17, 2003, E12.

135 **"We're getting better"**: Ibid.

"I'm loving it": "'Paradise' Found: Lewis Brings a New Attitude to Cincinnati," *Washington Post*, September 3, 2003, H13.

136 **"eerily similar to the 34–6 opening-day loss a year ago"**: Mark Curnutte,
"The More Things Change . . . Familiar-Looking Loss in Opener Deflates
Promise of a New Era," *Cincinnati Enquirer*, September 8, 2003, D1

"This is more like a marathon": Ibid.

"Hang with us, we'll be back": Ibid.

"Expectations are a lot higher than they've been": Mark Curnutte, "One
Step Forward, Two Steps Back?" *Cincinnati Enquirer*, September 18, 2003, B1.

"that is my responsibility": Mark Curnutte, "The Key Plays Go the Other
Way," *Cincinnati Enquirer*, September 22, 2003, D1.

137 **since 1978 had qualified for the postseason**: Ibid.

138 **"didn't scream, dance or do anything stupid"**: "Bengals Christen Lewis,
Themselves with First Victory," *Washington Post*, September 29, 2003, D9.

their strongest offensive performance since 1999: Sean Smith, "Lewis
Earns His Stripes—Bengals Coach Does Number on Old Team," *Boston
Globe*, October 20, 2003, D11.

their first two-game win streak in two years: Mark Curnutte, "Everyone
Joins in the Fun: Team Effort Gives Bengals Upset Victory over Seattle,"
Cincinnati Enquirer, October 27, 2003, 1D.

committing zero turnovers: Mark Curnutte, "Turnovers Lead to Triumph," *Cincinnati Enquirer*, October 20, 2003, 1D; Paul Daugherty,

"Confidence, Winning Going Hand-in-Hand," *Cincinnati Enquirer*, October 27, 2003, 1D.

138 **"recently arrived from another planet"**: Daugherty, "Confidence, Winning Going Hand-in-Hand," 1D.

"letting you have it for free": Mark Curnutte, "Winning Changes Everything," *Cincinnati Enquirer*, December 7, 2003, 1B.

139 **"In Marvin We Trust"**: Breanna R. Kelly, "30–10 Defeat to Denver Broncos a Dampener in Season Opener," *Cincinnati Enquirer*, September 8, 2003, 1A.

"overnight there were tulips everywhere": Tony Kornheiser, "These 4–8 Teams Are Half Bad," *Washington Post*, December 5, 2003, D1.

"The Greatest Show on Turf": Joe Giglio, *Great Teams in Pro Football History* (Chicago: Raintree, 2006), 37.

140 **"We've got more to do"**: "Crash from Past: Bengals Are Out," *New York Times*, December 29, 2003, 4.

"and pretty soon that tree will fall": Mark Curnutte, "'We've Got to Get Another One': With First Victory in Hand, Bengals 'Keep Chopping,'" *Cincinnati Enquirer*, September 29, 2003, D1.

141 **guidelines recommending what the FPA proposed**: The League's guidelines exempted situations in which teams filled positions with "persons within the organization" or "family members of team owners." Jarrett Bell, "Group Seeks Diversity in NFL Front Office," *USA Today*, March 7, 2005, 2C.

Chapter 10: Digging New Wells

146 **"Because they don't have buoyancy"**: ABC's *Nightline*, April 6, 1987.

"club presidents or presidents of banks . . . I don't know": Ibid.

"a prejudiced bone in his body": Jon Entine, *Taboo: Why Black Athletes Dominate Sports and Why We Are Afraid to Talk About It* (New York: Public Affairs, 2000), 233.

147 **"trained monkey working for [her] than a nigger"**: Shropshire, *In Black and White*, 23.

148 **"Well, you better hurry up and get to the airport"**: Author's interview with Kenneth Shropshire; author's interview with Kellen Winslow.

149 **"We drink from wells we did not dig"**: Author's interview with Kenneth Shropshire.

154 **"Negro Wall Street"**: Tim Madigan, *The Burning: Massacre, Destruction, and the Tulsa Race Riot of 1921* (New York: St. Martin's, 2001), 3.

Page screamed that she was being attacked: Ibid., 52–53. From the beginning, Tulsa police doubted Page's story, and Page eventually both dropped the charges and apologized to Rowland for the false allegations. Ibid., 234, 237.

155 **"get a gun and get a nigger"**: Ibid., 118.

155 **"Negro Uprising"**: Ibid., 117.

156 **"powerless individuals in and around Los Angeles"**: Author's interview with Charles J. Ogletree Jr.

   "not afraid to represent poor black people": Ibid.

   "epitaph should say, 'When people called, Johnnie would come'": Ibid.

Chapter 11: The Road to Super Bowl XLI

163 **flooded 80 percent of the city**: Jeremy I. Levitt and Matthew C. Whitaker, *Hurricane Katrina: America's Unnatural Disaster* (Lincoln: University of Nebraska Press, 2009), 2.

   sheltered more than thirty thousand New Orleanians: Ibid., 260.

164 **"This game's over"**: Dungy, *Quiet Strength*, 284.

165 **such a deficit in a conference championship game**: Michael Silver, "'It's Our Time,'" *Sports Illustrated*, January 29, 2007, 44.

   "We're going to win this game": Dungy, *Quiet Strength*, 284.

166 **"I'm very proud to be representing African Americans"**: Nancy Gay, "Two Teams with a Lot to Prove Heading to Miami," *San Francisco Chronicle*, January 22, 2007, D1.

   "first black coach to hold up the world championship trophy": Sam Farmer, "Historic Achievement Is Just Super for Smith, Dungy," *Los Angeles Times*, January 22, 2007, D7.

Epilogue

168 **propel him into his head coaching position with the Bears**: Smith has publicly stated of his head coaching position with the Bears: "I would like to think owners would hire the best coach but I'm here because of the Rooney Rule." Clifton Brown, "Bears Hope Takeaways Lead Them to a Title," *New York Times*, January 30, 2007, D2.

   diversifying the leadership ranks of the nation's art museums: Author's interview with Richard Lapchick.

   opportunity throughout the business community: Author's interview with Cyrus Mehri.

169 **for all of their athletic programs**: Oregon H. R. 3118, 72nd Leg. assembly, Regular Sess. (May 1, 2009).

172 **"intentionally savage"**: Judy Battista, "Secret to Steelers Coach Tomlin's Success: Take Notes," *New York Times*, January 26, 2009, D1.

INDEX

Pratt, Geronimo, and, 29
press conference of, 41–42, 47
race card and, 28
RCC and, 155–56
Simpson murder trial and, 28
success of, 117
Tagliabue, Paul, on, 110–11
Cochran, Johnnie L., Sr., 26
Cohen, Milstein, Hausfeld & Toll, 21
"Color on the Court" (Karabel & Karen), 185
Columbia Law School, 145
Combs, Sean, 153
Cornell Law School, 17
Cosby, Bill, 101
Coslet, Bruce, 35, 96
Cottrell, Ted, 105
Coughlin, Tom, 102–4
Court of Appeals for the Sixth Circuit, 81
Covington & Burling, 61–62, 74
Cowher, Bill, 160, 170
The Cubs: The Complete Story of Chicago Cubs Baseball (Stout), 176
Curnutte, Mark, 135–37

Dallas Cowboys, 17
head coaches of, 89–90
Parcells, Bill, and, 91–92
Dallas Morning News, 90
Daugherty, Paul, 138
Davis, Al, xi, 19
Shell, Art, and, 4–5
Davis, Timothy, 176
Davis, Willie, 75
Davis Cup, 45
Del Rio, Jack, 104–5
Denny, Reginald, 28–29
Denver Broncos, 135
desegregation, 176
of professional sports, 2
Detroit City Council, 114–15
Detroit Free Press, 107–8
Detroit Lions, 105
criticism of, 189
Detroit City Council and, 114–15
investigation into, 129–30
Mariucci, Steve, and, 107–9
Mornhinweg, Marty, and, 107–8
Rooney Rule and, 109–10
Wooten, John, and, 111–12
Diallo, Amadou, 99–100
Dillon, Corey, 137

discrimination. *See also* employment discrimination
customer, 84–85
Harper, Tommy, and, 36–40
in NBA, 83–85
second-generation, 15–16
against white players, 80
Winslow, Kellen, and, 75–76
District of Columbia Public Defender Service, 154
diversity
efforts, by NFL, 64–65
NFL meetings for, 56–58, 59–60
Owners' Workplace Diversity Committee and, 72–74
double standard, 19
criticism of, 79–80
statistics proving, 34–35
Douglass, Frederick, 28
draft picks
Cincinnati Bengals and, 131–32
forfeiture, in Fair Competition Resolution, 71
Wooten, John and, 54
Duffner, Mark, 102
Dungy, Tony, 125–26
2006 season of, 13
AFC Championship Game, 2006 and, 9–11, 164–65
on African Americans, 166
Anderson, Ray, and, 73
double standard for, 19
FPA award for, 149
hiring by Indianapolis Colts, 12–13
history of, 11
Landry, Tom, and, 18
on Lewis, Marvin, 103
as player, x
season of 2005 and, 159–60
Super Bowl XLI and, 1, 167–68
at Tampa Bay Buccaneers, 11–12
termination of, 18

Edwards, Harry, 59, 181
Edwards, Herman, 13, 161
Anderson, Ray, and, 73
EEOC. *See* Equal Employment Opportunity Commission
Elks Club, 37–39
emancipation, 25
employment discrimination, 21
statistics and, 21
at Texaco, 22